TEACH WRITING WITH GROWTH MINDSET

Classroom-Ready Resources
to Support Creative Thinking,
Improve Self-Talk, and
Empower Skilled, Confident Writers

DR. SARA HOEVE

Published by:
ULYSSES PRESS
PO Box 3440
Berkeley, CA 94703
www.ulyssespress.com

ISBN: 978-1-64604-313-2
Library of Congress Control Number: 2021947095

Printed in United States by Kingery Printing Company
10 9 8 7 6 5 4 3 2 1

Acquisitions editor: Casie Vogel
Managing editor: Claire Chun
Project editor: Renee Rutledge
Proofreader: Beret Olsen
Front cover design: Amy King
Cover art: © stmool/AdobeStock
Interior design: what!design @ whatweb.com
Layout: Jake Flaherty
Production assistant: Yesenia Garcia-Lopez

*This book is dedicated to my father, Paul Erffmeyer—
an incredible teacher and mentor who has always
believed in my potential for growth.*

CONTENTS

FOREWORD

Dear Reader,

As a former English teacher, I have witnessed firsthand the paralytic effect that a blank screen can have on an emerging writer. Absent the belief in your ability to create something uniquely informative, beautiful, powerful, or truthful through writing, that blinking cursor can feel like it's taunting you: *You can't write! Your ideas are terrible! You're going to look stupid!* But here's the thing: becoming a great writer is just like becoming great at anything else—it takes a lot of hard work, perseverance through failure, and, of course, the right mindset.

Mindset is a simple concept with powerful consequences. Boiled down to its essential meaning, growth mindset, on one end of the mindset spectrum, is the belief in your ability to improve through effort and perseverance. On the other end of the spectrum, fixed mindset is the belief that your abilities are fixed—that you were born with natural talent in a particular area or you weren't, and there's not much you can do to change that. And the way you approach a challenge or situation, whether with an open-minded willingness to grow or a close-minded belief that success is impossible, will lead to an outcome that reflects that mindset. To borrow Henry Ford's famous words, "Whether you think you can or think you can't—you're probably right."

That's it. That's the crux of mindset. After studying mindset in the classroom for six years and publishing five books on the topic, I realized that fixed-mindset beliefs account for many solvable problems in education. From school policies that underestimate students with learning challenges and limit access to advanced classes to students who resist a new opportunity, these damaging beliefs can topple dreams and level aspirations before they even have a chance to fully form.

Few subjects bring out students' fixed mindsets more than writing. Many students enter the language arts classroom believing that great writers are born, not made. That erroneous belief can prevent students from even attempting to hone their writing skills. This apathy—bolstered by the misguided notion that no matter how hard they try, they will never be any good—leaves students asking themselves, *"Why bother trying at all?"*

Students often spend their formative years laboring under the assumption that completing the first draft means the finish line is near and then feeling defeat and confusion when receiving critical feedback. Most people fail to understand that the first draft in writing is just the *beginning* of the process. Just as Michelangelo sculpted *David* from a block of marble, the writers' first draft is their metaphorical block of marble, waiting for the beauty within to be revealed through careful sculpting.

It would be nice if we could just reach into our students' brains and flip the growth mindset switch to the on position when it's time to write. If only we could make them believe that it is not a special God-given gift that makes a superb writer but the willingness to see a piece of writing through each stage of a complex process. Unfortunately, no such switch exists. The individual student, not the teacher, determines mindset when approaching a new challenge. So, what's a teacher to do?

Dr. Sara Hoeve answers this question in the following pages by reimagining the traditional writing process and the writing classroom. Instead of the finished draft being the goal, Dr. Hoeve's strategies focus on the *process* of writing in a growth-oriented environment. Her growth-mindset strategies for teaching writing shine a spotlight on feedback, editing, and rewriting—which, every accomplished writer knows, is where the magic happens. Focusing on encouraging iteration, delivering meaningful feedback, and developing a growth-oriented classroom culture, Dr. Hoeve outlines a process for getting your students to engage with writing like never before.

Once your students realize that writing is a process anyone can learn and the classroom is a safe space in which to explore that process without fear of judgment, beliefs about writing begin to shift. Together, you will eschew the rampant misconception that the first draft reflects the best ability and deepen your understanding of what it means to be a writer. Being a great writer isn't about being bestowed with some ineffable gift. Rather, it is a gradual building of skill. It is taking away and adding and changing and rewording until something extraordinary begins to emerge. It is the understanding that all polished masterpieces once began as rough drafts.

In our information-driven world, writing well is not a nice-to-have skill, it's a *need*-to-have skill. Every student should leave high school with the ability to express themselves clearly and confidently in writing. That begins by dismantling the fallacy that only a few "chosen" people can do it well. This book will help you create the conditions and implement the strategies necessary to help your students shed the false limitations of the fixed mindset and relish in the triumphs and opportunities of growing into skilled writers.

Annie Brock
Coauthor of *The Growth Mindset Coach*

INTRODUCTION

WHAT TO EXPECT FROM THIS RESOURCE

Teach Writing with Growth Mindset begins with a review of mindsets, examining Stanford psychologist Carol Dweck's research on the topic and its impact on the field of education. After revisiting mindset beliefs about intelligence, we will consider how teachers and researchers have applied the concept of mindsets to examine the beliefs and behaviors common to different student populations and disciplines.

The discussion then shifts to the central premise of this book: how the science of mindsets has unique applications for understanding and motivating student writers. In an effort to examine the role of writing mindsets, we will consider the parallels between previous research and common beliefs about the nature of writing, recognizing characteristics that often emerge from those beliefs and reflecting on the effects of those beliefs on our students—not only in the development of their skills, but in their identity as writers.

TEN STRATEGIES FOR FOSTERING A GROWTH-MINDSET CULTURE

In order to provide teachers with a resource that is easily accessible, the content in this book is divided into ten ready-to-use strategies:

1) Create writing goals.

2) Model the writing process.

3) Focus feedback on "next steps."

4) Provide equitable feedback.

5) Offer formative feedback during the writing process.

6) Share the importance of self-talk.

7) Build trust and community.

8) Recognize struggle as necessary for growth.

9) Make time for reflection.

10) Use growth-oriented assessment practices.

Although the strategies are organized in a sequence similar to the flow of a writing workshop, they do not need to be read in that particular order. Readers may select the strategies that they find most helpful or that will best meet the needs of the students in their writing classroom.

Each strategy opens with a central belief statement, identifying the way we can use a growth mindset lens to impact student writers. The subsequent paragraphs develop a theoretical framework for the strategy, identify the connections between growth-mindset theory and best practices in writing instruction, and analyze the ways in which the teaching strategy will impact the beliefs of student writers. By moving from ideas to action steps, this resource provides teachers with specific instructional tips, classroom activities, text suggestions, and student examples to guide the implementation of each growth-mindset strategy.

Teachers will also find additional resources, such as reflection questions, writing prompts, mindset surveys, discussion starters, and much more throughout this resource.

READY-TO-USE REPRODUCIBLE HANDOUTS

This resource also includes twelve reproducible handouts ready for use in any growth-oriented classroom. All handouts can be easily adapted for different grade levels or classroom settings. These handouts include:

1) Brainstorming My Writing Goal (page 140)

2) My Writing SMART Goal (page 141)

3) Individual Writing Profile (page 145)

4) Response Groups Assignment (page 148)

5) Talk Back to Fixed-Mindset Thoughts (page 151)

6) Verse Novel Project (page 153)

7) Growth-Mindset Personal Narrative (page 156)

8) Semester Self-Assessment (page 158)

9) Standards-Based Literature Assessment (page 160)

10) Personal Narrative Rubric (page 164)

11) Single-Point Rubric (page 166)

12) Writing Process Performance Rubric (page 167)

PACING

If there is one thing I know for certain, it is that there is no recipe for teaching. The decisions about our curriculum, content, and pacing must always be based on the needs of our learners and the context of our classroom. While this resource offers numerous activities and resources, it is not intended to add to your list of curriculum requirements. Providing students with feedback, modeling new skills, setting goals—many of these strategies are not new or surprising; in fact, you are probably using most of them in your instruction already! Instead, this book offers teachers an approach to help students recognize their unlimited potential as writers. By applying a growth-mindset lens, you can hone your strategies to increase your students' confidence in their own abilities as they move through the writing process.

Before you begin, consider your professional goals and identify the needs within your classroom. Then select the strategies that will best address those particular areas. For example, if you are frustrated by your students' efforts during revision, you might read through the strategies concerning teacher feedback. By trying a new method or adapting some of your current feedback practices, you may find your students becoming more invested in their own growth as writers.

Created for busy teachers, this resource provides strategies and writing activities that can be easily adapted and integrated into any classroom routine. Each chapter provides new tips and tricks to transform the culture of your writing classroom. After you implement this growth-mindset approach, your students will finally be ready to let go of the "bad writer" label!

CHAPTER 1

UNDERSTANDING GROWTH MINDSET

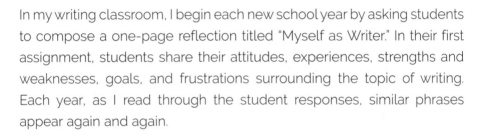

In my writing classroom, I begin each new school year by asking students to compose a one-page reflection titled "Myself as Writer." In their first assignment, students share their attitudes, experiences, strengths and weaknesses, goals, and frustrations surrounding the topic of writing. Each year, as I read through the student responses, similar phrases appear again and again.

- "I am a terrible writer."
- "I'm such a bad writer that I will be lucky to get a C."
- "I'm not a good writer."
- "I'll never get better at writing."
- "I've always been a bad writer, probably because my parents are bad writers too."
- "I know my writing is awful because I always get comments from my teacher."

If you were to step into any classroom across the country, you would likely encounter students who would make similar statements and share similar beliefs. Rather than viewing their moments of success and failure in the context of the learning process, they have used those feelings and experiences to construct a fixed identity. They are indicators of *who they are* as writers.

For many students, these negative writing identities have been created over time, shaped by their interactions with teachers and experiences in classrooms. Some students believe they are terrible writers because a teacher's red pen points out all of their grammar errors while ignoring their ideas. Many students struggle to find motivation to write about the topics they are assigned, while others see a low grade as proof that they'll never get better at writing. Too often, second language or nonstandard speakers encounter judgment or are labeled as deficient, incompetent, or "basic writers" by their peers and teachers. Over time, the "good writer" and "bad writer" labels have become part of student identities in most writing classrooms.

These writing labels, along with student beliefs about their own abilities, are vitally important, as they impact engagement and effort in classroom activities and writing assignments. Decades of research in educational settings show that a student's belief about their ability to write well has significant impact on their attitude, motivation, and actual achievement of the writing task. Those who see themselves as "bad writers" often give minimal effort or withdraw, wasting time or becoming overwhelmed by a writing task. They know they are terrible writers, so why would they keep trying if they will never improve? Why let classmates and teachers see their weakness?

In contrast, when a writer possesses a positive and strong writing identity, they are more inclined to invest in writing with passion and effort. Our confident writers bring in multiple drafts for additional feedback after school. They are eager and excited to try a new type of writing and expect that even if they struggle, they will eventually succeed. The student's writing identity influences the choices they make, whether to invest and engage in writing or to avoid it at all costs. Just believing that they are capable writers benefits students when they attempt to write, not because the belief itself increases their writing competence, but because it helps increase motivation for writing, sustained effort, and perseverance when obstacles get in the way of the task. The confidence that the student has in their own capability determines what they do with the knowledge and skills they actually possess.

Recognizing the massive influence that a student's beliefs and effort can have on their learning, and the important role teachers play in how most students view their writing, we must do everything possible to make sure that our classrooms cultivate positive writing identities for our students.

A THEORY OF MINDSET

One avenue for impacting writing identities can be found in the science of mindsets. The concept of growth vs. fixed mindsets, outlined in Carol Dweck's best-selling book *Mindset*, caused a major shift in the way educators think about student learning and intelligence. The growth-mindset belief system asserts that our personal abilities, such as intelligence, are malleable qualities and can grow or develop with persistence, effort, practice, and a focus on learning. In contrast, in a fixed-mindset belief system, people possess innate traits or aptitudes that are largely unchangeable.

Dweck and colleagues theorize that mindsets originate from people's beliefs about the fixedness or malleability of their personal qualities, such as their intelligence—that you either "have it or you don't," or you can cultivate it through learning and effort.[1] It is these two theories of self that create meaning systems which then go on to foster motivation and the use of particular strategies.[2] These strategies result in different levels of self-esteem, interest, and competence, especially in the face of challenge, failure, or threat.

We can measure these beliefs by asking people to agree or disagree with a series of statements, such as "Your intelligence is something basic about you that you really can't change," or "No matter who you are, you can substantially change your level of intelligence." Agreement with statements like the first one generally reflect an entity theory, which attempts to measure fixed abilities that remain consistent over time regardless of additional effort and support.[3] Those with fixed-mindset beliefs often feel that some kids just "get it" while others never will.

In contrast, agreement with statements like the second one reflect a malleable or incremental theory supporting the growth mindset. Those in this camp believe the new research about neuroplasticity, recognizing the brain's ability to expand with time and persistence. For them, every new challenge and task is an opportunity to learn and grow.

While Dweck's bestseller focuses on the role of mindset in the domains of business and athletics, her research on education found that mindsets can have a profound impact on the way students perceive and acquire new skills in the classroom. The beliefs a student holds about the nature of their abilities will directly impact their decisions, attitudes, and achievement.

According to Dweck and her colleagues, there is a direct correlation between a student's mindset and their academic success. When students believe they can control their learning, they are more motivated to work hard, while others fall into patterns of helplessness. The empirical data demonstrates that those with incremental or growth-oriented beliefs typically achieve greater academic achievement, while students holding an entity theory are less likely to attempt challenging tasks and are at risk for academic underachievement.[4]

For example, students who view their abilities as malleable believe they can increase their achievement through effort, persistence, and the necessary support. They respond to challenges by working harder, trying new strategies, and seeking out additional help. A growth-mindset educator understands that, with effort and support, all students can demonstrate significant growth, and, therefore, all students deserve opportunities for challenge. These beliefs serve as a foundation for a culture of success and student achievement in schools.[5]

While self-beliefs can be strong predictors of future academic performance and success, they are not necessarily enough to create success on their own; instead, the mindset is an important influence on the student's attitude, self-efficacy, motivation, and resilience, which, in turn, directly impacts subsequent achievement. It is necessary for the students to believe that their abilities are "grow-able" before they can utilize the new skills or strategies they have been taught.

In contrast, a student with fixed-mindset beliefs sees their intelligence as a set amount or number—like an IQ score—one that cannot be changed by effort or learning. These students are likely to draw conclusions about their ability from a setback or low score (e.g., that they are not smart), and then give up quickly to avoid effort and embarrassment. After all, what is the point in working hard if they will not be successful?

It is not only struggling students who show fixed-mindset thinking. Advanced and gifted learners can also possess fixed beliefs. They have likely coasted through school without exerting much effort, yet are praised for their high grades and strong skills. These students often struggle with great anxiety and become consumed with "looking smart" to the extent that they avoid risks or challenging tasks. Perceiving negative feedback or failure as a reflection of their intelligence (they are no longer "smart"), fixed-mindset students will blame outside forces and quickly disengage in the learning process. Because they have often succeeded quickly at most tasks, they also consider time as an important indicator of ability. For these students, any struggle is a sign of weaknesses, as they believe "smart" students learn a new concept or skill right away and without much effort.

The fixed mindsets of educators and parents can directly influence children's beliefs about their abilities or how they view themselves as learners.[6] Throughout various educational contexts, adults can communicate damaging mindset messages to students. When teachers or administrators determine that a class or activity is "too hard" or "not the right fit" for certain students, they stymie student potential by creating a knowledge ceiling, a certain level beyond which a student will never be able to advance. School structures driven by fixed-mindset beliefs eliminate opportunities, communicate low expectations, and prematurely remove students from challenging environments. Rather than evaluating student potential by standardized test scores or the pace at which work is completed, growth-mindset educators value the student's curiosity, effort, and drive.

The good news is that Dweck, along with her colleagues Lisa Blackwell and David Yeager, found that they could actually change students' mindsets through targeted interventions, and in turn, boost their achievement. When students learned through a mindset intervention that they could "grow their brains" and increase their intellectual abilities, they began to perform better. In addition, the researchers also used the interventions to teach students about key elements of the learning process, such as learning goals, hard work, and healthy responses to failure. The new learning strategies became part of the framework for growth-mindset beliefs, which was shown to increase the students' academic and social competence over time.

In the decade since the publication of *Mindset*, educational researchers have considered the implications of mindset theory on the behaviors and beliefs of students in various disciplines and grade levels, as well as those with socioemotional and cognitive needs. Many of these studies have been conducted in academic contexts that students perceive as difficult, such as learning math, transitioning to junior high school, beginning college, or studying a foreign language. Scholars have also evaluated the effects of mindset interventions on low income, high-risk, rural, and urban students. Additional studies have focused on the role of mindsets in academic success by examining students with high grades, as well as those with learning disabilities or receiving special education services. Other mindset interventions have been used on adolescents with anxiety, depression, and obesity. Researchers have also attempted to increase achievement through mindset interventions in Norway, Japan, the United Kingdom, Peru, France, Chile, and Argentina. Numerous teacher-centered books, along with countless journal articles and blog posts, have outlined ways in which educators can harness the power of mindset to motivate students, build their resilience, and ultimately, increase student achievement.

The influence of mindsets has also been widely researched across different academic domains, including reading, second language, music, art, engineering, science, computer programming, medicine, and math. In each case, researchers delineate discipline-specific characteristics and implications of mindsets, supporting the theory that mindsets and subsequent interventions can be content, task, or skill specific.

However, the research on growth mindsets is largely absent within writing education, limited to a handful of dissertations and one published study investigating how fixed mindsets affect students' writing.[7] While research has proved that mindsets are a pivotal factor for student motivation and academic achievement, writing teachers do not have a resource discussing the role of mindsets in writing processes, or how mindset interventions might encourage growth and increase efficacy in student writers.

Given the fact that so many people believe that one must have a "gift" for the "art" of writing, the role of mindsets seems particularly important for understanding a student's writing process. Building on the established body of research, this book uses a mindset lens to highlight the impact that self-beliefs have on a student's writing identity, as well as their motivation, engagement, and actions. By better understanding how mindsets impact student writers, teachers can identify the instructional strategies that will encourage growth and foster positive writing mindsets.

CHAPTER 2

STUDENT WRITERS AND THE SCIENCE OF GROWTH MINDSETS

While we recognize the importance of writing skills for college and career readiness, the statistics are dismal. In a 2011 article in the *Washington Post*, "Why Americans Can't Write," Natalie Wexler, chair of the Writing Revolution, reported that only about 25 percent of all students demonstrate proficiency in writing.[8] In comparison to 2011, the most recent national data from the 2017 NAEP Writing Assessment shows a pattern of even lower performance.[9]

In the face of these bleak numbers, we could point fingers and assign blame to over-testing, burned-out educators, inadequate resources, cultural biases, and more. And we would be right. However, we could also put our time and energy into gaining additional insight into the writing process of our students. What barriers are preventing their engagement with writing? How can we improve the proficiency of the writers in our classrooms?

In my pursuit of answers to these questions, I began focusing on the beliefs our students hold about writing and their abilities. The majority of research in this area centers on the writing self-concept or writing self-efficacy of a student, which the late researcher Frank Pajares defined as "the judgments of self-worth associated with one's self-perception as a writer."[10] Someone's writing efficacy reflects their beliefs about their own writing ability: *Am I a capable writer? Can I complete a writing task successfully?* Beginning in the 1990s and continuing until Pajares' death in 2009, research by Pajares and his colleagues dominated the field of writing self-efficacy and consistently showed that writing self-efficacy plays a critical role in students' writing process and impacts their writing performance.

Because of the relationship between writing self-efficacy and writing performance, beliefs about writing soon became a major focus in studies on student writers. In examining students' motivation, Bruning and Horn found that their beliefs about the nature of writing must be "sufficiently potent to carry the writer through the difficult and often emotion-laden processes of writing." These beliefs include one's competence as a writer, but also the perceptions that their writing has value and matters in the world. In their publication, the authors urged future researchers to consider other beliefs that students hold about writing, as they wondered: "Is there, for example, a parallel to the belief structures identified by Dweck and Leggett (1988), where some students take an entity view of writing, assuming that their writing ability is largely fixed?"[11]

In response to that call, University of Porto, Portugal faculty Teresa Limpo and Rui Alves became the first researchers to study children's implicit theories of writing, which comprise the fixed- or growth-minded beliefs students hold about the malleability of their writing ability. Just as Dweck had considered one's beliefs about the nature of intelligence (Can I grow my intelligence?), Limpo and Alves examine one's beliefs about the nature of writing (Can I grow my writing ability?). Limpo and Alves coined the term "implicit theories of writing," referring to learners' beliefs about the nature of writing, and they argue that teachers should be "mindful of students' beliefs as well as nurture incremental views of writing."[12]

Three years later, Laurel Waller and Mostafa Papi examined the incremental theory and entity theory of writing intelligence. While the incremental theory refers to learners' "belief that writing intelligence is dynamic and can grow through effort and experience," entity theory means that they hold a "belief that writing intelligence is fixed and unchangeable."[13] Phrases to assess learners' entity theory of writing intelligence include: "You can improve your English writing skills, but you can't really change your writing talent," and "As an English learner, you have a limited amount of talent for developing your English writing skills, and you can't really do much to change it." We can clearly see that items in their assessments were derived and adapted from Dweck's research on implicit theories about intelligence.

Writing teachers know that many students believe they are incapable of becoming strong writers. These beliefs could stem from a number of factors, such as their personal backgrounds, teachers' appraisals, or even the confidence their parents have as writers. However, the beliefs may also form when students view writing as a gift or talent that one has either been given or withheld at birth.[14] Michael Palmquist and Richard Young consider the potential effects of this entity view in their study on giftedness: "Students who believed more strongly that writing ability is a gift tended to have (a) higher levels of writing apprehension and (b) lower self-assessments of their ability as writers."[15] Since one's implicit beliefs directly influence one's actions and performance, mindsets likely play a significant role in students' choices and their success with writing.

As educational research has shown that students' mindsets are critical to their learning and achievement, teachers should begin by investigating whether their students hold fixed or growth-minded beliefs about their writing ability. In *Opening Minds: Using Language to Change Lives*, Peter Johnston emphasizes the importance of our language choices and how our words can often reflect our mindsets about learning.[16] By listening to the ways our students talk about themselves as writers, we can begin to identify the orientation of their writing mindset beliefs.

MEASURING WRITING MINDSETS

Researchers have offered a few different scales to measure student mindsets. Limpo and Alves's scale to measure implicit theories of writing asks students to indicate their level of agreement with the following statements: "My texts will always have the same quality, no matter how much I try to change it"; "No matter how many texts I write, their quality will always be the same"; and "I can't change the quality of my texts."[17]

In 2015, SUNY Old Westbury Associate Professor Nicole Sieben first presented her validated Writing Mindset Scale (WMS), which was later published in *Writing Hope Strategies for Writing Success in Secondary Schools*.[18] The Sieben Writing Mindset Scale includes eight statements that are rated using a six-point Likert scale ranging from strongly disagree (score: 1) to strongly agree (score: 6). Some of the statements reflect fixed-mindset beliefs, like "Your writing ability is something that you cannot change very much," and "You have a certain amount of writing talent, and you cannot really do much to change it." However, Sieben's scale includes additional statements that reflect growth-mindset beliefs, such as "You can always substantially change how much writing talent you have" and "No matter who you are, you can significantly change your writing ability." For these statements, "disagree" answers would indicate fixed beliefs about writing.

At the time Sieben was validating her scale, I was creating my own WMS for my research on a writing mindset pedagogy.[19] Sieben and I include one identical item on both of our scales: "Your writing ability is something that you can't change very much." In addition, statements #1 and #3 on my scale are quite similar statements in Sieben's validated WMS.

HOEVE WRITING MINDSET SCALE (2018)

Directions: Please take a moment to read each sentence below and mark the choice that shows how much you agree or disagree with each statement by choosing the number that corresponds to your opinion.

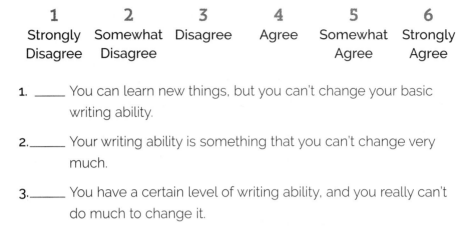

1	2	3	4	5	6
Strongly Disagree	Somewhat Disagree	Disagree	Agree	Somewhat Agree	Strongly Agree

1. _____ You can learn new things, but you can't change your basic writing ability.

2. _____ Your writing ability is something that you can't change very much.

3. _____ You have a certain level of writing ability, and you really can't do much to change it.

A WMS or similar survey is a useful tool for determining your students' mindsets about their writing abilities. The more a student "agrees" with the first three statements in the above survey, the more their answers represent fixed-mindset beliefs about writing. Greater levels of disagreement indicate a greater presence of growth-mindset beliefs.

Mindset scales can help us determine a student's beliefs about the nature of their writing abilities—whether they view writing as a fixed talent or a malleable skill—and understand the ways in which the student reacts to struggle, frustration, and feedback within the writing process. These belief systems may provide reasons why certain students demonstrate resilience, show optimism, and try out new strategies, while other students become quickly discouraged, avoid risks, or give up easily. Furthermore, mindset scales may provide us with important information for classroom interventions, as they offer a means of assessing the impact of growth-oriented instructional strategies on our students' beliefs and identities.

WRITING MINDSET CHARACTERISTICS

Students who recognize the potential to grow or develop their writing abilities view their writing abilities as malleable skills that can be increased through effort and support. These growth-minded students recognize their potential as writers and see their effort as meaningful. Aware of their own agency, these writers may show more optimism, less writing anxiety, and less apprehension. Growth-minded writers enjoy being challenged, viewing it as an opportunity to learn.

In addition, students with growth-oriented beliefs will likely be able to struggle and fail without losing the confidence to try again, showing resilience in the face of difficult tasks. Grasping the importance of effort, these writers are able to respond to setbacks by remaining involved, seeking out more feedback from others, trying new strategies, and using all of their resources. According to Frank Pajares and Margaret Johnson, positive writing self-beliefs can be strong predictors of future academic performance and important motivational factors because they impact "the choices [students] make, the effort they expend, the persistence and perseverance they exert when obstacles arise, and the thought patterns and emotional reactions they experience."[20]

In contrast, if students' statements about "not being good writers" reflect fixed mindsets, these beliefs will likely undermine their performance and their enjoyment of writing. Fixed mindsets can be limiting for students when they believe in the innate nature of their writing ability, viewing it as an unchangeable quality. This notion assumes that good writers will always have success in writing, and the terrible writers will continue to fail regardless of their actions or effort. A fixed-minded writer would believe that their writing skills could not be significantly developed, much like someone who says "I'm not athletic," or "I can't do math." With this mindset, students often believe that if they aren't naturally talented or don't catch on right away, they might as well give up. If they believe that they cannot alter or increase their writing skills, they will have little motivation for learning new strategies and will likely have negative attitudes toward the writing task. Their negative internal self-talk will loop on a fixed-mindset script: "I'm just a terrible writer," "Writing is not one of my strengths," or "There's nothing I can do, I will never be good at writing." When a teacher or peer offers feedback, fixed-mindset writers feel easily discouraged and defensive to the critique. They do not recognize the role of effort or view writing as a skill to learn.

While we may assume fixed-mindset beliefs are held by students who fall below proficiency, high achievers often subscribe to an entity theory as well. However, these beliefs are harmful for students at both ends of the spectrum. For the students who struggle or do not perceive themselves as "good writers," the negative identity becomes a self-fulfilling prophecy. Because they don't really believe that they can be successful, they will often give up quickly or avoid a writing task altogether. However, the fixed mindset also poses problems for those who sincerely believe they are "good writers." Looking smart becomes their top priority. This results in students avoiding any writing that requires risk or holds the potential for failure, preferring instead to stick with formulaic structures or cliché topic choices as they aim for perfection or "error-free" writing.

In addition, the writing mindset will likely impact the student's perception and reaction to feedback and process. If "good writing" is an innate quality, they would likely believe that a "good writer" would be successful immediately, with little need for teacher feedback or multiple drafts. Fixed writing mindsets may view peer or teacher feedback, drafting, and revising as indicators of their failure. Imagining that "good writers" find quick success on the first attempt, they may resist the writing process, feeling defensive and dejected by any teacher suggestions, interpreting the best writing as the one with the least amount of teacher comments.

Characteristics of Fixed- vs. Growth-Minded Writers

FIXED-MINDED WRITER	GROWTH-MINDED WRITER
Anxious and apprehensive about writing, as they believe their past struggles indicate poor ability	Less apprehension and anxiety about writing since they are continuing to learn and grow
Views writing success as out of their control	Believes that effort can impact achievement
Avoids writing tasks that require risk or skills in which they lack confidence	Responds to risk or difficult tasks by remaining involved, trying new strategies, and using resources
Likely to give up in the face of difficulty and challenge	Shows resilience and grit in the face of difficulty and challenge
Underestimates their ability	Overestimates or accurately estimates ability
Uses negative self-talk about their writing ability	Chooses positive self-talk and "yet" statements
Values looking smart over learning	Values challenge as an opportunity to learn
Does not care to explore topics or ideas in depth	Able to think critically and reconsider assumptions
Low on self-accountability and self-assessment	Demonstrates metacognition throughout the writing process
Tries to hide weakness by blaming others	Tries to understand weakness in order to improve ability
Threatened and frustrated by feedback on writing	Seeks out feedback from teacher and peers
Does not value revision, prefers to write "one-and-done"	Values revision as necessary for growth
Interprets failure as an absence of ability	Able to fail without losing hope

Characteristics of Fixed- vs. Growth-Minded Writers	
FIXED-MINDED WRITER	**GROWTH-MINDED WRITER**
Pessimistic when beginning new or unfamiliar writing cycles	Optimistic when beginning new or unfamiliar writing cycles
Gives minimal effort in writing tasks	Gives best effort in writing tasks
Believes good writers write "right" the first time	Sees writing as an ongoing process, with many struggles and successes
Views writing ability as an innate talent or gift, which they are given in a set, unchanging amount	Views writing ability as a malleable skill, which they can grow over time with effort and support

WRITING DISPOSITIONS

Many of the characteristics of fixed- and growth-minded writers correlate with thinking dispositions, or "*habits of mind*," as outlined in the "*Framework for Success in Postsecondary Writing*."[21] Published by the Council of Writing Program Administrators (CWPA), the National Council of the Teachers of English (NCTE), and the National Writing Project, this framework outlines learning outcomes for college writing assignments, as well as eight dispositions, or "ways of approaching learning," that support students' success in college and career. According to experts from the CWPA, NCTE, and the National Writing Project, these habits of mind, which include curiosity, openness, flexibility, and persistence, are necessary attributes of successful writers.

Mindsets are especially evident when students encounter difficult challenges and struggle with writing, such as when they are responding to failure, managing conflict, and overcoming negative stereotypes. This is when their internal dispositions and self-beliefs must be strong enough to carry them through the difficult and often frustrating process of writing. In addition to having persistence and flexibility, students must believe that they are capable of a successful writing performance.[22] This belief benefits a student when they attempt to write an essay—not because the belief itself increases their writing ability, but because it helps create a better attitude toward writing, inspire more effort on the assignment, and increase perseverance and grit when frustrations and anxiety arise. The confidence that the student has in their own capability helps determine what they will do with the knowledge and skills they actually possess.

In order to foster positive dispositions, students must first understand writing as a malleable, learnable skill. If they hold tight to writing as a fixed, innate ability, they will not find the motivation to be persistent or open to engaging in new challenges. As teachers develop a deeper understanding of writing mindsets, they can better identify instructional strategies that target internal beliefs and communicate that writing is learnable. It is only when we create and support a growth-oriented writing environment that we can nurture positive dispositions and give students the confidence to achieve goals, accept feedback, and persevere through setbacks.

CHAPTER 3

GROWTH MINDSET IN THE WRITING CLASSROOM

Once we recognize the power of mindsets, we can begin to target our students' beliefs about writing, their understanding of their own abilities, and their engagement in the learning process. It is encouraging that early research on writing mindset interventions shows that teachers and tutors do have the potential to alter the mindset beliefs of student writers.[23] However, it will not be enough just to teach students about fixed and growth mindsets toward writing. Instead, we must build a classroom community that values effort, creativity, and flexibility, focuses on the process over product, and, above all, celebrates the students' growth as writers.

LEARNABLE COMPONENTS

Before we dive into the writing process, we must first address the students' underlying beliefs about the nature of writing. We can start by asking our students to consider their abilities. Do they believe that they can become talented musicians, artists, or athletes with time and hard work? Or do they believe that these abilities are gifts that only a select few possess? If one has the ability to paint or sing or dribble, will they always be successful on the first or second try? What many of our students do not realize is that each of these abilities contains a number of *learnable components*, aspects of an ability that can be learned through time, effort, and support. Although I may not possess the natural skill of Adele, LeBron, or Tiger Woods, I can focus on the learnable components of singing, basketball, or golf. Although I cannot sing, paint, or play golf very well with little to no training, it does not mean that I can't gain those abilities with effort, time, and support.

In order to effectively teach the learnable components of writing, we must first target the writing mindsets of our students, making sure students understand that writing is a malleable or growable ability. If a student believes that they will always be a "terrible writer," no amount of lesson planning, conferencing, or writing practice will make much difference in their writing process. Instead, they will just be moving through the assigned steps in order to complete a paper or earn a high grade. Even if students learn effective skills or strategies for their writing processes, they may not fully employ them adequately unless they possess a mindset that believes in their potential to grow their abilities.

PURPOSEFUL PLANNING

Although teachers can and should explicitly teach students about the science of mindset and the nature of writing, it takes a lot of purposeful planning to create a growth-mindset culture in the writing classroom. Our writing instruction must be organized through a mindset lens as we communicate fixed- and growth-oriented messages through our teaching strategies, writing feedback, assessment practices, and even our classroom décor. All aspects of the writing process should echo with growth-mindset messages!

To create a classroom culture that values growth, teachers must truly believe that all writers can be successful. This belief is essential to creating the sort of space that helps a writer develop a positive identity and growth-oriented beliefs, as the mindset of a teacher contributes greatly to the likelihood of a student's success. If a teacher does not believe in the student's potential for growth, not much else will matter.[24]

When you implement a growth-mindset approach, students will begin to see writing as a skill, one they can continue developing with effort and support, much like practicing for a basketball team or learning a musical instrument. This approach to writing emphasizes the importance of growth over correctness, process over product, and persistence, effort, and even failure in our development as writers. As consistent teacher and peer feedback, goal setting, and self-assessments offer new information for self-efficacy beliefs, the students' understanding of writing as an innate quality of who they are shifts to a skill they have the ability to change.

This new culture also supports other cognitive elements of the writing process, including motivation, writing confidence, metacognition, and healthy responses to failure. By targeting student mindsets, teachers aim to increase the effort and persistence students devote to a writing task, their willingness to try new strategies, and their receptiveness to instruction and feedback. As students gain confidence and positive attitudes, they are better able to achieve goals, embrace challenge, and recognize their growth as writers.

THE QUESTION OF ENVIRONMENT

While mindset interventions have the potential to disrupt or alter fixed-minded beliefs, they do not remove the adversities in a student's environment. Moreover, mindset interventions are not a substitute for systemic efforts to alleviate racism, poverty, and economic inequality. Teachers should not interpret the emphasis on effort as an encouragement for students to "pull themselves up by the bootstraps."

However, mindset interventions can be used to alter students' understanding of their own potential and, in this way, they may combat the psychological inequalities that can impact achievement and future opportunity, especially negative labels and stereotypes. In many educational environments, students of color are stereotyped as lower in intelligence, and girls are stereotyped as less successful in STEM subjects. In situations where these stereotypes are present, students are more likely to feel inferior, and even just the reminder of negative labels may cause them to doubt their abilities and impact their achievement. Concerned about the risk of confirming a negative stereotype, known as "stereotype threat," a student's performance can decrease when they identify with a negatively stereotyped group.

The good news is that teaching students about the growth mindset has been shown to reduce the likelihood that they will be influenced by stereotype threat.[25] Stereotypes are similar to fixed-mindset beliefs, as they imply that an attribute or ability is fixed—some groups have it and some don't. However, a growth mindset contradicts these stereotypes with the message that even if a person is struggling, they can do better in the future with more effort and additional support. Students who lack privilege are not inferior or incapable; instead, with the opportunities, tools, structures, and time for learning, they too can achieve success.

In an extensive study of public schools in Chile, Dweck and colleagues collected data from tenth-grade students to examine the impact of socioeconomic background on student mindsets. Similar to the stereotype threat, they found that economically disadvantaged students were more likely to hold fixed-mindset beliefs than their wealthier peers, as the lowest-income Chilean students were twice as likely to report fixed-mindset beliefs about their abilities. However, when students from low-income families did hold a growth mindset, their academic performance measured as high as students in the 80th income percentile. The researchers concluded that possessing a growth mindset may actually buffer students from the effects of poverty on achievement.[26] Rather than denying the profound impacts of environmental influences or structural inequalities, mindset theory can help illuminate factors within the student's control that can be more readily changed.

Many major school reforms in the United States today address structural factors such as the size of the class, the quality of the teachers, and the length of the school day, or they attempt to directly teach students remedial skills for studying, developing vocabulary, reading, and writing. These efforts are undoubtedly important, but they rest on the assumption that students are not learning or engaging because they have not been given the correct resources or classroom environment. Mindset theory proposes that student beliefs about the nature of their abilities may prevent them from fully taking advantage of those resources. As a result, an intervention to address mindsets can offer a new avenue for building writing resilience and motivation, and lead to long-term effects on student achievement.

Mindset interventions challenge the determinism of fixed-ability categories by shattering the myth that some students are inherently smarter, more talented, or better than others. At the same time, we must be careful that we do not imply that success is solely dependent on individual effort. Instead, mindsets are one way to target student beliefs and increase achievement, while also helping to defeat myths and stereotypes about students' potential.

SELECTING MINDSET STRATEGIES

While the 2016 national survey "Mindset in the Classroom" showed that 98 percent of teachers overwhelmingly agree that growth-mindset approaches should be adopted in schools, only 50 percent said that they knew of specific strategies to effectively change a student's mindset.[27] The study found that "there is a great hunger for more and more effective training," as 85 percent of teachers want more professional development related to growth mindset.

My goal for this book is to share specific strategies to help you harness the power of mindsets for writing instruction. If students can accept that all writers can grow their abilities, they can dive into the writing process with confidence rather than obsessing over an error-free product or feeling defeated after an unsuccessful attempt. As teachers, we encounter opportunities every day to encourage growth-mindset beliefs in our students. Let's look for ways to encourage effort, normalize failure, and increase resilience during the writing process!

PEDAGOGICAL GOALS

Create a growth-mindset culture for writing by using a variety of strategies and classroom practices that communicate and reinforce the importance of growth. A teacher with growth-oriented beliefs about writing should hold the following pedagogical goals:

- ✓ Expectations are high for all writers because the instructor believes all students have unlimited potential for growth.
- ✓ Responsive, differentiated feedback meets the developmental needs of each student.
- ✓ Modeling shows how experienced writers move through the writing process, break down complex problems, solicit feedback from others, and revise, revise, revise.
- ✓ All students have the opportunity to engage in tasks that offer "next steps" challenges.
- ✓ Students have a conceptual understanding of writing as a skill, and the role both effort and failure play in their growth as writers.
- ✓ Students explore many different strategies, resources, and approaches to find the ways that best support their writing style.
- ✓ Opportunities for goal setting and reflection are embedded into the writing cycle.

✓ Writing happens within a safe community, where struggles and successes can be shared and celebrated.

OPENING REFLECTION QUESTIONS FOR TEACHERS

Before exploring the growth-mindset strategies, take time to reflect upon your own beliefs and attitudes about mindsets, writing instruction, and a positive classroom culture. Use these prompts as a starting point to begin thinking about the nature of learning, as your instructional choices and classroom practices will likely derive from these beliefs. You can jot down answers on your own or discuss them with colleagues. These are complex questions, so don't worry about producing correct answers or even addressing every question.

- If I truly prioritized the growth of my student writers, what would my classroom look like? What would my teacher feedback sound like? What would my grading look like?

- How could I allow, even encourage, failure and reward hard work?

- Do my students currently feel safe enough to task risks and make mistakes in my classroom? What evidence supports my answer?

- What are my fixed- and growth-mindset beliefs about my own learning and abilities?

- How do I find time to give each student meaningful, individualized feedback, pointing out areas for growth as well as *how* to improve in that area?

- How can I provide critical feedback that does not harm my student's confidence?

- How do I train students to provide more meaningful, growth-oriented feedback to one another?

- What might be ways to incorporate more self-assessment and reflection into the feedback process?

- How do I encourage or support the students who are defensive or dismissive of feedback from others?

- What mindset messages am I currently sending through my feedback and assessment?

- Do any of our school practices or policies limit a student's potential?

CHAPTER 4

STRATEGY #1: CREATE WRITING GOALS

> **CENTRAL GROWTH-MINDSET BELIEF:** Goal setting *communicates* an underlying belief that students *can* and *will* grow as writers.

In a growth-mindset classroom, we believe that our students' writing abilities can be developed with continued effort and support. Perhaps one of the most important ways to do this is by helping them set meaningful goals for their writing and monitor their progress toward achieving those goals. Simply by asking students to set writing goals, you communicate a central growth-mindset belief: you *can* improve and *will* expand your current writing abilities. After establishing the classroom expectation that we can grow as writers, you can then guide students in setting new, personalized writing goals, choosing the most effective writing strategies and supports, and navigating through the setbacks.

Goal setting allows students to develop agency and choose the direction for their learning. Opportunities for choice can increase students' intrinsic motivation, allowing students to put forth effort in ways that they want to, not that the teacher has assigned. However, students must believe that their efforts are not in vain—that the more they commit to developing their abilities, the closer they will come to achieving their writing goals. By empowering students through goal setting, you promote autonomy, purposeful learning, and mastery in writing development.

When a student sets specific, challenging, yet attainable goals, they are more likely to see improvement in performance than if they are just "doing their best." The planning steps are also important, as the student must determine the specific strategies, steps, and support needed to meet the desired goal.

Deliberate, goal-directed writing practice is an essential component of a growth-oriented classroom and can be incorporated throughout the school year. We can invite students to create a Specific, Measurable, Actionable, Realistic, and Timely (SMART) goal, one that spans a specific unit or an entire semester.

We can also include smaller goals that address a shorter span of time—perhaps setting a word count they want to hit by the end of the week, or aiming to add strong dialogue in their narrative writing. By allowing students to create self-directed goals, they begin a writing phase from a place of confidence and success, increasing their writing efficacy and emphasizing that they can grow their writing skills.

By targeting one or two specific areas, you can help make writing success feel more attainable to students. Too often, my student writers define "good writing" as getting everything "right." When I ask them to explain a little more, they provide a lengthy list of grammar and mechanical rules: complete sentences, no spelling errors, transition words in each paragraph, commas in the correct spots, and on and on. If students take the time to create concrete and meaningful writing goals, they can focus on specific skills that will develop their abilities as writers, rather than feel overwhelmed by the pressure of writing "right" on the first try.

Additionally, the end of a large project or unit can be a great time to consider new goals. Rather than viewing a final grade as a fixed indicator of their intelligence or ability, students can use the teacher's end comments and rubric to evaluate the success of the strategies they used and identify new areas for growth in their next writing phase. After our last paper cycle, a few of my students created new goals focused on their writing habits, such as writing for a certain amount of time each day or finding a quieter place to work. Others addressed specific writing strategies, setting a goal to visit the writing center or prewrite before beginning a draft. When students were not sure of a new goal, we reviewed their rubric together and identified possible areas for growth.

Goal setting becomes an essential part of maintaining a growth mindset throughout the writing process. Without a concrete idea of what we want to achieve and a plan of how we're going to get there, it's easy to slip back into a fixed mindset when we encounter an obstacle. A growth mindset that embraces the challenges of writing will continue ahead, push further than expected, and not be discouraged by failure. In this way, goals become part of our ongoing process as writers. When we meet a goal, we have not reached the destination, but merely passed a mile marker in our journey of growth.

ACTION STEPS

1) Encourage Students to Set Daily, Weekly, Unit, or School-Year Goals: In order for students to take ownership of the writing process, they should begin to create their own personalized writing goals stemming from regular reflection and discussion with the teacher, and then revisit these goals during individual writing conferences. Consider having students set larger SMART goals (see below) to track throughout the school year, while creating smaller, more informal goals for a writing prompt, daily work time, or research assignment. Smaller goals can help keep students focused and accountable during independent work time, or they could be used to target new skills that provide the scaffolding necessary for achieving their larger SMART goals.

- Reproducible #1: Brainstorming My Writing Goal (page 140).
  Using this handout, ask students to begin considering their writing by jotting down their strengths, frustrations, resources, and future

goals in the four large boxes. Under the boxes, students will find a continuum line #0–10, where they can indicate or rate their current writing abilities. This handout introduces students to the metacognitive thinking that we want to encourage throughout the writing process. It also begins laying the groundwork for thoughtful goal setting, as students have an opportunity to take an inventory of their current writing abilities.

2) **Use Visualization to Help Increase Writing Efficacy:** According to social cognitive psychologist Albert Bandura, self-efficacy is a strong indicator of performance, motivation, and well-being.[28] One way to increase self-efficacy is through visualization, or *imaginal experiences*. By imagining yourself performing well in a task that you have to accomplish or behaving effectively in a given situation, you can gain confidence in your own abilities. Through the process of setting writing goals, your students can begin to imagine their future successes, which reinforces and strengthens the belief that writing success is possible.

In order to build these growth-oriented beliefs, start a new semester with writing prompts that invite students to picture their successes in your writing class. A short writing assignment like the First Week Writing Notebook Prompt not only anticipates the student's successes, but requires them to identify specific writing strategies or work habits that will contribute to that success. Therefore, this prompt increases efficacy and introduces the process of setting writing goals.

EXAMPLE: First Week Writing Notebook Prompt

Write two paragraphs under the title "How I Earned an A in This Course." Imagine that you are writing this on the last day of the semester, after you have finished the final project, and you have just seen an "A" as your final grade. In the two paragraphs, explain how you earned your A. In your reflection, consider the course requirements, the resources offered here at school, as well as your own successful strategies for reading, studying, planning, writing, and time management. If you have not always practiced successful strategies and habits, you may have to give this some thought or even look up strategies that would help you in areas that have typically caused you trouble. (Procrastination anyone?)

3) Review Past Achievements and Growth: While many sources can contribute to a person's self-beliefs, Bandura identifies past "mastery experiences" as holding the greatest influence.[29] Performing a task successfully strengthens our sense of self-efficacy, as it provides evidence of our capabilities. However, failing to adequately deal with a task or challenge can undermine and weaken self-efficacy. Whenever students begin a new class or assignment, they can feel positive or negative emotions based on their prior experiences, which influence their actions and impact their successes.

To help build confidence and encourage growth-minded thinking, ask students to reflect on past successes and ways they have already grown as writers. Perhaps they could share writing assignments they completed in previous grades or areas that they used to find difficult but now find easier. As a sixth grader, my son struggled to write three or four complete sentences for an assignment; however, he can now produce two pages of writing in just one class period of his high school English class. His writing stamina and ability to generate ideas have greatly improved over the past five years. When I remind him of his resilience and growth as a writer, he feels confident that he has what it takes to succeed.

4) Help Students Distinguish Between Performance Goals and Learning Goals: While both types of goals can help boost achievement, students should reflect on the purpose behind their goals. Performance goals—which focus on demonstrating tasks, content knowledge, or skills—provide a measure or validation of one's ability, often in relation to others. In contrast, learning goals focus on understanding and growth, with an emphasis on improving or mastering skills when facing obstacles or new learning challenges.

Since performance goals often focus on short-term achievement, they can align with fixed-minded beliefs, especially when students assume that they would meet those goals through natural talent and quick success. Instead, learning goals recognize the role of sustained effort and grit, helping to foster a growth-oriented mindset about our writing abilities.

In *The Growth Mindset Coach*, Annie Brock and Heather Hundley offer a lesson plan for exploring learning and performance goals with students.[30] The lesson plan includes an activity in which students can identify the purpose of a goal as *learning goal* or *performance goal.* In the chart below, I offer a similar activity for students; however, in this version, students are asked to evaluate goals that are specific to the writing process. This exercise serves as a resource to help students understand the difference between a writing goal that aims for growth and understanding versus one where performing well is the main objective. When students can clearly discern the difference, they are better equipped to set high learning goals focused on discovering new knowledge, skills, and strategies. Rather than aiming to write an "A" paper or meet a certain word requirement, our students will create goals to better understand and navigate through their writing process.

Learning vs. Performance Writing Goals

	LEARNING GOAL	PERFORMANCE GOAL
I will figure out how to identify good research sources for my project.	X	
I will work on giving helpful feedback to my peer writing group.	X	
I will look at model short stories to understand how to add sensory details into my narrative essay.	X	
I will get a perfect score on my vocabulary quiz.		X
I will be able to recognize and fix run-on sentences.	X	
I will get zero wrong on my grammar test.		X
I will use my teacher's feedback to revise and improve my paper.	X	
I will get the highest grade in the class.		X
I will finish my essay first.		X

5) Develop SMART Goals: Using the SMART structure helps students to create meaningful goals that are realistic but challenging enough to require effort and persistence. Additionally, SMART goals contain a clear time frame and measurable action steps so they can track progress and make adjustments if necessary.

Typically, my students start by creating vague goals for their writing:

I will do better in my writing this year.

In order to make the goal SMARTer, they must revise their goal to make it specific, measurable, and realistic:

I will do better in revising my papers this year.

We still need to add timely action steps for a truly attainable SMART goal:

I will revise each writing assignment at least once this semester after seeking out feedback from my teacher and peers.

- Reproducible #2: My Writing SMART Goal (page 141) offers a template for your students to create long-term SMART writing goals for the semester or school year.

6) Suggest Strategies to Remain Gritty!: As students begin to pursue their writing goals, they are likely to encounter obstacles and frustrations along the way. When this happens, you have the opportunity to promote grit. In the best-selling book *Grit*, psychologist Angela Duckworth identifies grit as an indicator of success in nearly every domain. She found that this combination of perseverance and sustained passion is just as important as intelligence or talent when it comes to achieving a goal.

In order to evaluate a student's potential for success, examine their reactions to a challenge. Do they show persistence and effort, or do they give up quickly? According to Duckworth, grit comes from a cycle of what she calls "deliberate practice," which begins with a *stretch goal*— setting an appropriate challenge, committing 100 percent to attaining that goal, getting feedback, and then reflecting on the feedback to refine their practice as needed. It is this cycle of deliberate gain, rather than natural ability, that leads to expertise and success.

When students create meaningful writing goals, you can support them by holding individual writing conferences, suggesting strategies, and providing timely feedback. The student will use your feedback to direct their revision, and after reflection, they will create new writing goals for the future. By providing ongoing coaching and feedback, you have the opportunity to encourage grit and offer resources that support students as they face setbacks during the writing process. Rather than giving up quickly when facing a challenge, writers can continue to grow by getting gritty with continued persistence and effort.

Writing can be difficult and painful, even in the best circumstances. One of the benefits of goal setting is it provides us an opportunity to anticipate the challenges ahead! Once we identify the potential potholes, we can gather strategies that will keep us on the path to success.

For example, my students often place the blame on writer's block when they start to feel drained or overwhelmed during the writing process. However, if they could anticipate this obstacle while setting their writing goals, they could create a plan to keep moving forward. Rather than giving up when they feel stuck writing, they can turn to their strategies and remain gritty!

EXAMPLE: Writer's Block Strategies

✔ Read (and RE-read) the instructions from the assignment.

✔ Free-write for 10 minutes about anything, just to get your creative juices flowing.

✔ Lower your standards to just generate ideas, not to write it "right" the first time.

✔ Use a thesaurus to add variety in your word choice.

✔ Make a list to generate new ideas.

✔ Ask your teacher questions that focus on your specific frustrations.

✔ Experiment by rearranging the current order of your paragraphs.

✔ Read a model text to see examples from other authors.

✔ Cover your computer screen with a piece of paper while typing.

✔ Draw a visual representation of your ideas using pictures or symbols.

✔ Take a break or a walk outside.

You may also notice your students employing fixed-mindset language when they encounter challenges and start to feel frustrated. When you hear this negative self-talk, respond with growth-minded questions that redirect the student's focus to possible strategies and solutions for moving forward.

Fixed Frustrations vs. Growth-Minded Questions	
WHEN THEY FEEL LIKE STOPPING...	**OFFER GROWTH-MINDED QUESTIONS TO POINT TO A PATH FORWARD**
Something went wrong!	How can you use this mistake to improve your draft?
I already wrote it once! I don't want to start over!	How can use this feedback to make your writing even stronger?
I don't know what to write!	What writer's block strategies have you tried?
I hate my first draft!	Who can provide you with feedback?
I hate all these writing rules!	How can you clearly present your ideas to your readers? What will your readers expect?
Creating citations is just so hard!	How will you practice getting better? Where can you find helpful resources?
My paper won't be the best!	What does mastery look like for you? What are your writing goals?
I don't know what to write about!	How have you found successful ideas before?
This assignment is too easy!	How can we build in a just-right challenge for you?
I'm finished writing!	Where to next? What are your future goals?

CHAPTER 5

STRATEGY #2: MODEL THE WRITING PROCESS

> **CENTRAL GROWTH-MINDSET BELIEF:** By modeling the writing process, teachers increase student confidence and promote positive mindset messages.

An important component of a growth mindset is the student's belief in their ability to be successful. If students do not believe that they can succeed, they resist putting in the time and effort needed for growth. Instead, they are likely to demonstrate fixed-mindset traits, like avoiding challenges and giving up quickly. Modeling is one of the most effective ways to increase a student's confidence in their own abilities, as the learner is able to visualize a clear pathway to success by way of the teacher's example.

Just as we turn to older siblings, coaches, or favorite celebrities as our role models, teachers can also serve as inspiration for success in certain skills or learning goals. When students observe a successful model, this vicarious experience increases their efficacy and motivates them to also perform well. According to Bandura, "Seeing people similar to oneself succeed by sustained effort raises observers' beliefs that they too possess the capabilities to master comparable activities to succeed."[31]

In order to encourage growth-minded thinking and boost student confidence, teachers can integrate successful models throughout the writing process.

In the writing classroom, modeling provides students with an opportunity to observe someone else performing a writing task successfully. When modeling, explain the writing strategy you will use, demonstrate the strategy in front of the students, and then explain why you chose to use that particular strategy. While observing your process, students will compare your actions to their previous writing experiences. For many students, this comparison can be a powerful influence, as they realize that they already possess many of the skills and strategies necessary for success. The teacher's model helps students construct positive perceptions of their own competence, as they begin to feel "I can do that too!" By building confidence in your students' abilities through the act of modeling, you increase efficacy and foster growth-minded thinking in the writing classroom.

The use of modeling can be practiced in two different ways. First, teachers and peers can model the *process* of writing by demonstrating a skill, sharing their writing process or problem-solving strategies through a *write-aloud*. Second, teachers can provide students with a model of a writing *product,* such as a mentor text or peer sample.

MODELING THE PROCESS

In whole-class mini-lessons, you can present a powerful model for students by working through a portion of your own writing in front of a class, or by sharing your experiences as a writer. Take your students through a how-to demonstration of each step of a particular strategy, such as revising a paragraph or creating a thesis statement. It is important to talk aloud in order to share the interior thinking and decision-making process of an experience writer. This practice also provides an opportunity to model your engagement with your own words and ideas as you give students a glimpse into the complex cognitive process of drafting, revising, editing, and reflecting.

Another option is to model problem-solving strategies by recalling your past successes and failures. Since I was teaching a composition course during the process of my dissertation, I frequently discussed my writing experiences with my students. When they began their research project, I described how I had divided parts of my paper into smaller, manageable tasks. When they began their revision, I showed my students the feedback from my committee and explained the many changes I made from one draft to the next. During that semester, we shared our stressors and celebrated together when our final drafts were submitted.

Although they can learn so much from teacher models, students also need opportunities to observe and discuss the writing process of their peers. It is reassuring for students to see that other students struggle with writing as well. Rather than becoming discouraged, students can help one another by sharing different problem-solving strategies. In a growth-oriented classroom culture, students and teachers collaborate as they offer a different point of view, suggest new approaches to a problem, or just share the energy of the writing experience.

MODELING THE PRODUCT

In addition to modeling the writing *process*, provide models for a writing *product*, such as mentor texts or peer examples. As a young teacher, I often felt frustrated when my students would fall short of my expectations for a writing assignment, especially after I had provided clear directions through a checklist or a rubric. Many times, I would even read the guidelines aloud to my students, explaining and elaborating on each requirement. Eventually, I realized that it was more helpful to share examples of a finished product, rather than explaining each one of the instructions. If we want students to write a convincing argument with reliable evidence, we must provide examples of writing with a clear claim and strong support. If we want them to craft a descriptive narrative, filled with dialogue and concrete details, we need to start by showing them an engaging story. Models provide students with a clear understanding of the success they can achieve.

In conversations with fellow teachers, some express concern that their students will just copy or imitate the model texts. In order to avoid this, we must spend time processing the mentor texts as a class, rather than just distributing the examples and moving on. In a close reading of the text, we can work together to deconstruct the unique features that make the piece a great example of writing. It is important to note, with all types of product models, that we are not just asking students to label these examples as "good" or "bad," but to instead dig deeper into the text. Rather than just provide students with our analysis of a piece, we encourage them to do the thinking by asking questions about the author's craft: *What choices is the author making? How are those choices impacting the text? How effective is the author in achieving the purpose of the text?*

By analyzing the "writing moves" the writer has made in a model text, we focus on *how* they have used language to create an effective piece. To make sure that students still produce original and creative thoughts, they should then take time to practice with their own writing in a low-stakes environment, one where they can take risks and explore new ideas without fear of grades or judgment. By providing models of both the writing process and writing product, you can increase student confidence, inspire new ideas, and encourage a growth-oriented approach to writing!

ACTION STEPS

1) **Process Model through a Write-Aloud:** During a write-aloud, verbalize your internal dialogue as you use a specific strategy, write a particular type of text, or narrate the metacognitive process involved in the writing process. Research shows that experienced writers possess

many strategies that are not used by novice writers, and students may learn a new cognitive strategy just by hearing your thoughts.[32]

In addition to providing a successful example, teachers achieve credibility as writers and create a more authentic community when we write with and in front of our students. Rather than planning out each of your steps beforehand, I would encourage you to use new or unfinished writing. Even if you feel a little uncomfortable with this idea, your unscripted process will be more realistic. By showing students that even their teacher's writing process can be messy and frustrating at times, we give them permission to struggle as well. Additionally, as you write in front of your students, you can model growth-mindset dispositions of curiosity, problem-solving, open-mindedness, and a willingness to accept feedback from others.

Select a writing strategy or technique that will allow you to display your thinking throughout the writing activity. Ideally, the strategy will address an area that often presents a challenge to your students, who will be able to use the strategy in many different writing contexts. During your write-aloud, share your passion for writing but also allow students to see the frustration and struggle that is a natural part of brainstorming, drafting, and revising.

EXAMPLE: Possible Write-Aloud Topics

How do I add engaging dialogue?

What types of images do I use in my presentation?

How do I insert quotes from my research?

Where do I find reliable research?

How can I structure a claim and evidence?

How do I write a great introduction? Or conclusion?

What ways should I use ethos, pathos, and logos?

How do I paraphrase a research article?

How do I outline my essay?

> How can I identify and strengthen weak word choices?
>
> What do I change to add more sentence variety?

If you have not used a write-aloud in your classroom, I have included the steps that I use in my own lessons.

Write-Aloud Steps

- When you model, begin by explaining the writing strategy and why you would use it. The *why* is important because we don't want students trying to force a certain strategy into every writing assignment (like the struggle we have had with the five-paragraph essay). Tell students that you will be verbalizing your own thinking for them as you write. Ask them to pay attention to the decisions you make as you write and ask them to begin thinking about their pieces in this way.

- Introduce the type of text you will write and what you hope the reader takes away from your writing.

- As you write, display your text on chart paper or on a document viewer, and then make verbal statements that describe your own decision-making while you write. It is important that you "show don't tell" during the demonstration, thinking aloud as you give students a glimpse into your writing process and making it clear that writing takes work.

- Make sure that your model isn't too rehearsed or planned out. You do not want your students to think that the writing process is easy for you. Otherwise, they will become more frustrated when they turn to their own writing and try the technique. I might show my struggle to find the right phrase or a sentence order that clearly captures my ideas. Showing your work helps to normalize the struggle involved in writing as something even adults face. You are also subtly reinforcing a growth mindset when you show the effort and work required in your process.

- After you have finished the write-aloud, invite students to share what they noticed about your thinking during the activity. What seemed to be important to you as you were writing? How did you problem-solve or make a decision?

- In a later class, invite students to share their own thinking during the writing process, or ask a student volunteer to try a write-aloud in front of the class. The class could then compare and contrast your write-aloud with the process of their fellow student.

In the sample below, I revised a recent draft of a poem for my students. Notice how the write-aloud incorporates problem-solving skills to encourage grit and persistence, as well as positive self-talk to reinforce our growth-mindset principles. This type of modeling is especially effective when it is built into a mini-lesson. After you have explained and modeled a technique, the students have time to dive back into their own writing.

EXAMPLE: Write-Aloud Poem

Today we are going to continue revising our person poems, which are helping us to think about choosing great details and powerful words, so we are able to communicate our ideas clearly in our limited amount of words. Since we have already completed our brainstorming activity and early draft, today we are going to work on our first revision. My person poem describes my relationship with my dad, and how it has changed—and continues to change with time. Let's start by reading through my current draft. As I read, I'm going to underline places that I'm still unhappy with or add my thoughts in the margin.

My Poem

For as long as I can remember, I was a daddy's girl.

We owned a special connection,

like a precious secret you confide in someone close

My Notes

Do I like the word *owned*? I want to use a better word than just *had,* but I'm not sure *owned* works. I'll use the thesaurus to see what better options I can find.

My Poem	My Notes
Because I was the oldest, and my mother took care of the babies	"Fish in the river" doesn't seem to fit with my repetition pattern here of "a deposit, a game..."
I would travel everywhere with dad	
A deposit at the bank, fish in the river, a game at Wrigley Field	
I was always along for the ride	
But—	I'm using the "But—" to show the transition, but I'm not sure if it's too much. Could I do something more subtle? I want to ask my writing group for their thoughts.
as I grew older, I became bored.	
I spent the rides staring out the window	
picking at strings on the car seat cushions or	
flipping through songs on the radio stations	
We never talked about the canyon expanding between us,	I'm worried this makes me sound boy crazy, like I'm looking for many men. LOL. I think I'll soften it a little, maybe 'finding someone younger to hold my hand."
as I sat and imagined running away	
I ached for freedom	
and finding new younger men to hold onto my hand	
Eventually—	I'm not sure about these verbs—although that's how it felt at the time. I'm going to ask my writing group what they think.
I ventured out in the world	
was chewed up and vomited out	
The prodigal daughter,	
dad welcomed me home	
Now—	I tried something new in this paragraph because I just sort of strung together these two sentences without using a period and I also indented the last line in a different way to set it off.
I feel claustrophobic	
panic choked me last week	
when I see my dad growing older and gray	See? I think it should be the past tense of saw...
attending the funeral of one of his friends	

Now that I've gone through my draft, I can see some areas that don't feel right. During our independent writing time, I plan to use my thesaurus and try out some different word options for *owned, chewed up,* and *vomited*. I also plan to brainstorm a list of other places that I went with my dad (church on Sunday, school in the morning, paint store, etc.) to see if I can come up with another example to take the place of "fish in the river." To be honest, my dad never even really took me fishing. I just liked the nostalgic image of a child fishing with her dad. After our writing time, I plan to share my revised poem with my writing group to get their feedback on the changes. I also want to hear what they think of my last paragraph, since I don't feel 100 percent comfortable with the way I broke the "rules" of writing. I want to check to see how that style impacts the way my readers interpret the last paragraph. After I do my own revisions and meet with my writing group during workshop today, I think I'll be close to a final draft for submission! I'm excited to finish my poem and share it with my dad. I wonder if he felt some of the same changes that I felt growing up.

2. PROCESS MODEL: INVITE STUDENTS TO PARTICIPATE IN SHARE-OUTS

Share-outs provide a great opportunity for students to share the decisions they are making in their writing with the rest of their class. These sessions occur when the teacher asks a particular student to describe a part of their writing process, such as how they came up with the idea for their introduction, or where they found the best resources for their research project.

A sharing session is particularly effective when it emerges from a student's writing conference. Jamal came to his writing conference struggling with ways to incorporate more "show, don't tell" descriptions into his narrative essay. Together, we identified some powerful points in his story where he could pause the action and add details describing his internal feelings and physical reactions. In the last ten minutes of class, I asked Jamal to share-out this development with his classmates. First, he read the original paragraph, in which he had struggled to describe his experience. Then he shared the revised version with his new "showing" details. Following Jamal's share-out, many other students were eager to return to their own essays, excited about the new ways they could improve their descriptions as well.

3. PRODUCT MODEL: INCORPORATE MENTOR TEXTS

When introducing new writing skills, mentor texts can be great resources to help students brainstorm ideas and demonstrate conventions we are asking them to use. You can use mentor texts to highlight the features of a specific genre, such as poetry, argument, or my narrative example below. However, they may also be used to highlight a certain skill— perhaps creating a strong thesis, formatting a letter, or using APA citation style. When working with mentor texts, we are asking our students to employ critical thinking skills by evaluating someone else's writing and making connections to their own.

In the beginning of a unit on narrative writing, I want to immerse my students in examples of powerful storytelling, so I select models that skillfully demonstrate features of the genre. Narrative mentor texts, often published professionally, are helpful when we discuss the genre features, talk about the writing "rules" (and, just as importantly, when we can break those rules for effect), and analyze the moves the writer makes in the piece. First, I read a narrative text aloud to the class, pausing at times to explain a word or share a technique that I have noticed. I "cold call" by selecting students at random to read different paragraphs or respond to a part of the text, as this keeps them engaged and focused on our reading.

After we finish the reading, I invite students to discuss three key features of the narrative text:

1) the organization of the timeline

2) the most powerful sensory details and dialogue

3) concrete descriptions that they could picture in their own imaginations

After we notice and discuss the first text's narrative features, students read a second narrative text and discuss the same features in that piece. Finally, they read a third narrative on their own and evaluate the same three features in their writing notebooks. Analyzing these three narrative texts, along with a few brainstorming activities, can be enough for some of my students to jump into their own writing. Other students spend additional time with other narrative models that I have collected in an online folder. They skim through the stories, diving into the topics that catch their interest.

When we begin working in our peer writing groups, the students have the language to discuss the narrative features that they notice in their classmates' papers. When I listen to the discussions, I often hear them referencing one of the model texts as they compare the different writing styles or recommend that their partner try a technique from another narrative essay.

EXAMPLE: Narrative Mentor Texts and Discussion Questions

Mentor Texts for Narrative Essay Unit

"Indian Education," Sherman Alexie

"Shame," Richard Gregory

"What's in a Name?" Henry Louis Gates Jr.

"Momma, the Dentist, and Me," Maya Angelou

"The Story of an Hour," Kate Chopin

"Learning to Read," Malcolm X

"Eleven," Sandra Cisneros

"Shooting an Elephant," George Orwell

"A Plate of Peas," Rick Beyer

"A Hanging," George Orwell

Questions for Students to Discuss

What moves and techniques employed by the writer make this a powerful narrative?

Compare two of these narrative essays. How do the authors develop different writing voices through tone and word choice?

Choose one area where the author uses a lot of great descriptions. Why was this moment of the story important?

How does the author choose to structure the time line of events? How does that impact the story?

---

4. PRODUCT MODEL: PEER-TO-PEER MODELS

In addition to mentor texts, it is important for students to examine the work of other student writers. For each of the larger writing assignments that I assign, I keep a folder of submissions from my previous students. When teaching a course for the first time, I have borrowed writing samples from my colleagues as well. These pieces provide my current students with a concrete understanding of the assignment and help them to begin to see different directions for their writing.

According to my students, the peer writing models often feel much more approachable and less intimidating than the mentor texts, which are mostly written by a teacher or a published author. These sample writings can serve other purposes as well. Students can discuss and evaluate the writing together, developing their peer feedback skills without the discomfort of the writer sitting across the room. The teacher can also place a few sample papers alongside the grading rubric, reviewing the rationale for the scores of each paper, in order to help the current students better understand the expectations of the assessment.

CHAPTER 6

STRATEGY #3: FOCUS FEEDBACK ON NEXT STEPS

> **CENTRAL GROWTH-MINDSET BELIEF:** Teachers can individualize their feedback by pointing to specific areas of growth and challenge for each student writer.

Finding ways to individualize feedback is essential to fostering a growth mindset in the writing classroom. In order to meet the needs of all learners, provide differentiated feedback that recognizes each student's strengths while making sure all students feel sufficiently challenged. A growth-minded approach assesses the current skills of each student and offers appropriate challenges through next-steps feedback.

As teachers, our mindset beliefs can affect how we respond to the needs of our students. If you truly believe that all students have the potential to grow as writers, you will give each student just-right challenges, high expectations, and the support necessary for growth. If we truly believe that abilities can be developed, we will take time to provide responsive feedback based on the unique needs of our student writers.

How can we give feedback in a manner that leaves our students excited, challenged, and prepared to revise? In my classroom, I direct my students to *next steps*—two or three focus areas that will help move their current writing skills to the next level of mastery. Rather than trying to "fix" everything possible, this provides my students with clear direction and concentrates on the high-value areas that will allow them to grow as writers in my class.

A focus on next steps can help us strike a balance between too little and too much feedback. When I highlight two or three next steps for every student, even my strongest writers feel challenged during revision. At the same time, I am offering an amount of constructive criticism that is manageable, rather than overwhelming, for my struggling writers. Most importantly, I am communicating growth-oriented messages about revision and feedback. In my classroom, all writers (including me!) need feedback that challenges us, followed by time for meaningful revision work, in order to continue growing our abilities. When we show students that we value revision, they will grow to value it too.

If you stepped into my classroom during workshop time, you would see my students working on a variety of skills and steps in the writing process. A couple of students will be rearranging their paragraphs, while another student will be gathering more research to support their thesis. Other students might be trying new techniques of craft as they select stronger word choices, brainstorm options for the introduction, or look up APA citation guidelines. While their attention may be moving in different directions, my role as the teacher remains consistent: to assess each of my student writers and provide them with the feedback necessary for growth.

Adam, a high school senior, explained how his high school writing teacher provided him with next-steps feedback:

> *Mr. J. knew each of us really well as writers, and he pushed us in different areas. Like, he encouraged one of my friends to put more of himself in his writing, but for me... he helped me work on clarity in my sentences. There were overall themes we all learned about writing, but individually, he motivated each of us to work on different areas. That type of feedback helped me become clearer with my ideas and my purpose.*

The combination of hard work and appropriate challenge levels can create the perfect conditions for facilitating growth mindset, as long as teachers are providing the appropriate support and encouragement for each student's writing needs. Individualized feedback and praise offered throughout the writing process can be powerful motivators for continued effort and perseverance. By using next-steps feedback to meet each student's needs, teachers communicate growth-oriented values about writing, encouraging their writers to embrace challenge and enhance their growth mindsets.

CONSIDER!

Are all of my students being challenged in their writing? Have I pre-assessed my students to identify which students have already reached mastery? Have I differentiated instruction so that all students have areas of growth?

How am I praising students who are taking risks and overcoming challenges in their writing? What writing supports and models are available to help the students when they get stuck?

ACTION STEPS

1. MONITOR EACH STUDENT'S INDIVIDUAL NEEDS THROUGH PRE-ASSESSMENT

The initial stage in next-steps feedback involves pre-assessment, in which you gather information to assess the student's current abilities and needs. Start by examining a writing sample, and then use that data to plan appropriate feedback for the student. You can collect data from previous essays, low-stakes writing activities, early drafts, surveys (which can indicate current mindsets, attitudes, motivation, or efficacy), writing goals, student reflections, individual conferences, or your observations.

While analyzing these materials, create data records to track student needs and growth. A writing profile like Reproducible #3 identifies the student's current strengths and struggles as a writer. In a growth-oriented classroom, you could also add data on the student's mindset beliefs, motivation, and attitudes toward writing. It is important to note that data collection should always be done in a living document, with new observations and updated assessments added as students continue to grow during the year. Each student's profile can assist you in recommending next steps, selecting appropriate feedback, and providing instructional supports in order to increase achievement and encourage growth.

- Reproducible #3: Individual Writing Profile (page 145) offers an example of a document to collect data for a student profile. One document would be used for each student in order to create a comprehensive writing profile and record the progress of student writing goals (noted early, in the middle, and at the end of the semester), mindset indicators (also noted early, in the middle, and at the end of the semester), your analysis of the student's writing samples, and your notes on one-on-one conferences.

2. OFFER NEXT STEPS TO PROVIDE ALL WRITERS WITH OPPORTUNITIES FOR GROWTH

Once you have identified the student's needs through pre-assessment, you are ready to differentiate your feedback by offering an appropriate level of challenge and responsive support. In order to make sure all writers receive personalized feedback, many teachers meet students for individual conferences during workshop time. In these meetings, the teacher acts as a writing coach as they ask questions and engage in conversation with the writer, gathering insight into which suggestions and supports might be the most helpful.

Individual conferences also offer a time to provide students with feedback on their goals, model a skill, or teach a new strategy. Each student in your classroom should receive this level of individualized attention, from the strongest writers to those who struggle the most. All students should be challenged to grow as writers.

Since I try to fit in five to eight writing conferences in each class period, I need to be prepared and direct when talking to each student about the next steps. I usually ask students to turn in writing on Friday, giving me two or three days to read through the drafts, making notes in the margins that will help guide my students in their revision. In addition, I note the next steps and highlight a few sections that I want to point out to the student. These notes will help direct my in-class conference with the student. Since I already have my notes prepared, I can conduct quick five-minute conferences with each of my students in two to three days. In the example below, I provide a summary of my next-steps conference with Vanessa.

EXAMPLE: A Writing Conference with Vanessa

In my first-year writing course, Vanessa has chosen to write her narrative essay about the first concert she attended with her dad. I approach Vanessa by checking in, asking, "How's it going?" She rolls her eyes in exasperation. I ask her to tell me where she is running into trouble. Scrolling down her screen, she shows me how she has added two more pages to her essay, explaining, "I just don't know how to cover everything that happened!" I quickly glance at my next-steps notes and see my underlined note: *Focus on purpose!* I can see that Vanessa is struggling with which details to include and which to leave out of her story, and the overall purpose is getting lost in all the details. I ask Vanessa, "How would you describe the main point of your essay? What do you want your readers to really understand?" She thinks for a movement, and then responds, "I want to show how my first concert really gave me a passion for music and was a special moment for me and my dad." "Then," I tell her, "we have to cut out the details that don't matter and give more attention to the sections that show that purpose."

As she listens, I show her, "Here, you describe getting ready in the morning. You woke up late, ate Cheerios, grabbed coffee with friends. That section takes up over a page of your essay, and it doesn't matter to your purpose at all. It has nothing to do with your passion for music. Now look at this section. You describe when the band takes the stage and you are surrounded by the screaming fans, the lights flicker, and the bass starts to beat. You feel goosebumps as you see the huge grin on your dad's face. *This* is the really intense moment when you are connecting with the power of music. *This* is the section to focus on and develop for your reader. You did the right thing by including all the details you remembered in your first draft. You needed to do that to get to all your deeper memories, so it was valuable and important for your writing process. But now you need to cut anything that doesn't support your central purpose."

When Vanessa turns in her next draft, it is half the size but twice as powerful. She is proud to show her new draft to her peer response group, who point out specific changes they like as well. This short conference with Vanessa, which lasted no more than five minutes, gave her a next step for her writing, providing a clear direction for revision and a path toward continued growth.

Our pre-assessments can help us determine readiness for each student. After considering whether a student is a beginning, developing, or advanced writer, we can select the next steps that provide the highest value, as we want to target areas that will have the most impact on their writing skills. In addition, we can suggest next steps that are often helpful for English language learners (ELLs). I have listed common next steps that I frequently use for students based on readiness. It is important to note that ELLs are not "below" beginning writers. In fact, second language writers may meet the readiness levels of developing or advanced writers.

Example: Next Steps Based on Readiness	
English Language Learners	Addressing issues with spelling
	Developing a better understanding of sentence order
	Learning about verb tense
	Clearly communicating ideas
	Understanding expectations about plagiarism and academic property
Beginning Writers	Finding and revising sentence fragments and run-ons
	Focusing on specific issues with punctuation and capitalization
	Developing paragraphs
	Communicating a clear purpose
	Organizing main and supporting ideas
	Using clearer, more specific wording
	Meeting format requirements of font, margins, and spacing

Developing Writers	Developing a strong thesis
	Communicating a clear purpose
	Using effective topic sentences and transitions
	Providing strong evidence
	Understanding formats for source citation
	Creating variety in sentence structure
	Using strong verbs
	Remaining consistent in tone and focus
	Starting with an engaging opening sentence or introduction
	Ending with a satisfying conclusion
Advanced Writers	Taking risks by breaking the "rules" (e.g., chronological order, interior dialogue, implicit ideas, etc.)
	Using humor or sarcasm
	Experimenting with the hyphen, dash, colon, and semicolon
	Strengthening voice and tone
	Including powerful concrete details
	Using concise and precise wording
	Finding writing contests and publishing opportunities

3. INCORPORATE ASSET-BASED GUIDING QUESTIONS

As you provide feedback on a specific piece of writing, give students specific suggestions or strategies to use in their revision. However, you can also ask guiding questions to help facilitate the student's thinking and to better understand their writing process. Look at the writer's process: why, how, and what your student writers do. Keep one or two of these guiding questions in mind when you approach a student for a conference.

If you haven't already used a mindset lens to examine the types of questions that you ask, now is a good time to start. These questions should never be threatening or judgmental, as you want students to feel safe and open to new ideas or pathways for revision. Avoid deficit-minded guiding questions, like "What is wrong with your thesis statement?" and use asset-minded questions, like "What have you learned about strong thesis statements?" Also, focus your guiding questions on the writer's process, rather than a specific product or outcome.

In the example below, you will find asset-minded guiding questions appropriate for many different skills, in both content and craft. A list that includes a wide variety of guiding questions will allow you to select the questions that best meet the needs of the student writer.

EXAMPLE: Asset-Based Guiding Questions

Organizing an Early Draft: Tell me why you decided to put your ideas in this order. What other ways could you organize this writing? How might it read differently if you changed the order? How have you organized your main and supporting ideas?

Clearly Communicating Ideas: How are you paying attention to your audience throughout your writing? What is the central idea of your second paragraph? Where could you add a couple more sentences to make sure your readers clearly understand your point?

Selecting Strong Word Choices: Which word choices are you most proud of? Are there any word(s) that you feel like you're repeating? Which passive or dull verbs could we replace with stronger action verbs? Are there sentences where you could use concrete language in place of an abstract idea?

Writing Precisely and Concisely: Which words could be removed without changing your meaning? How can we communicate the most meaning in the fewest words?

Hooking Readers in an Introduction: How can we make connections between your paper's purpose and your reader's life? Is there a story or anecdote that illustrates your point? What type of introductions make you want to read more?

Providing a Satisfying Conclusion: What do you hope your readers do or feel after finishing your piece? How can we emphasize your purpose in this final section? What ideas might give your readers a sense of closure?

Engaging Readers in a Narrative Story: Where could you slow down the story to build suspense? Is there a place we could add dialogue to communicate more emotion?

CHAPTER 7

STRATEGY #4: PROVIDE EQUITABLE FEEDBACK

> **CENTRAL GROWTH-MINDSET BELIEF:** Teachers must give substantial feedback to all students in order to establish revision as a necessary part of the writing process.

On a Monday morning in a writing classroom, John sits nervously as his teacher begins handing back the first drafts of their essays. John notices that Becky, a straight-A honor student, has received only a couple comments from the teacher on her essay. She beams, confident that her first draft was close to perfect. Next, John watches as the teacher hands an essay to his friend Noah—a paper that is covered in crossed out words, scrawled notes, and red ink. Noah crumples up his paper and shoves it deep into his backpack. He looks dejected and overwhelmed by the number of mistakes he will need to fix.

Inexperienced writers, especially students like John, perceive teacher feedback as an indication of their writing ability. They believe that "good writers" get writing "right" the first time, while "bad writers" have a lot of mistakes they need to fix. Teacher feedback and the need for revision become punishment for poor performance. When teachers make revision optional, or only require the step for struggling writers, they reinforce these beliefs.

In addition, an overwhelming wave of corrections and comments can destroy a writer's confidence, especially if they possess fixed beliefs about their ability (I must be a pretty terrible writer). Error-focused, "fix-it" feedback damages the writing identities of our students, as it communicates that getting better at writing is only about correcting mistakes. Rather than fostering growth, it turns the writing classroom into a high-risk, punitive environment.

In truth, all writers have more to learn about writing, and writing is not often done right the first time. Revising is not an indicator of poor writing or weak writers but the opposite—a sign and a function of skilled, mature, professional writing.

In a growth-minded classroom, teachers must establish the expectation of revision by building time into a writing process and providing a substantial amount of feedback for *all* students. If teachers commit to giving feedback to all students, they stress the importance of revision for growing as writers, regardless of the level of writing proficiency indicated in their drafts. This approach encourages the students to view feedback as a tool for growth, rather than a way to measure their ability.

In the classroom example above, the feedback approach instilled fixed-mindset reactions in both Noah *and* Becky. Not surprisingly, the teacher's feedback discouraged and overwhelmed Noah, causing him to just give up, rather than engage in meaningful revision. However, the lack of feedback also does a disservice to Becky, as she came to see feedback and revision as things to avoid, rather than the truth: effective feedback and revision are critical elements of the writing process.

THE DANGERS OF FIX-IT FEEDBACK

One of the most important aspects of a growth-minded classroom is the feedback stance of the writing teacher. When we read over a student's early draft, our first instinct as English teachers is to point out the grammar, punctuation, and spelling errors. Too often, our "fix-it" feedback is limited to these simple errors rather than the ideas, organization, or voice of the writing. By handing back the draft for students to "fix," we communicate that revision is only about correcting grammar and mechanics.

This "fix-it" approach to teacher feedback greatly limits the revision process for our stronger writers. When students like Becky do not receive feedback on their writing, they equate successful writing with "writing it right" on the first attempt. However, providing challenge on an individual level, especially for advanced writers, is critical to developing a growth-oriented classroom culture. Students must experience both the joy and struggle that come with a challenging task in order to buy into growth-mindset beliefs and develop the qualities of perseverance and grit. All writers need opportunities to push further than their current capabilities: to struggle and fail, then try again. If our more confident writers merely coast from one five-paragraph essay to the next, they will likely fall into fixed-mindset beliefs, believing that they are good writers because they can quickly and easily succeed without much effort.

Teachers have used this "fix-it" approach so often that most students have also adopted this limited understanding of revision. In my first four years of teaching, I would set aside at least two days for revision in just about every unit of the semester. On the first day, students would participate in peer editing. My instructions to the students were brief: "Today I want you to exchange your paper with your partner, read it carefully, and write notes on areas for revision." When Richard Straub spoke to novice writers about peer editing, he perfectly captured my students' approach as well:

> *You've got a student paper you have to read and make comments on for Thursday. It's not something you're looking forward to. But that's alright, you think. There isn't really all that much to it. Just keep it simple. Read it quickly and mark whatever you see. Say something about the introduction. Something about details and examples. Ideas you can say you like. Mark any typos and spelling errors. Make your comments brief. Abbreviate where possible: awk, good intro, give ex, frag. Try to imitate the teacher. Mark what he'd mark and sound like he'd sound. But be cool about it. Don't praise anything really, but no need to get harsh or cutthroat either. Get in and get out. You're okay, I'm okay. Everybody's happy. What's the problem?[33]*

Insecure about their own writing ability, many of my students didn't feel comfortable telling another writer to make a correction or revise a section. Since the editors saw themselves as "terrible writers," they feared that their "fixes" might make their friend's paper even worse. By the end of the day, most papers had a few additional commas and a couple of vague compliments, but not much meaningful feedback.

Following the lackluster peer-editing session, our second day was dedicated to revision. Again, I provided limited instruction, only directing the students to revise their rough drafts. Unable to recognize the weaknesses in their writing, the students felt lost and put little effort into their own revision. At the same time, the feedback from their peer-editing sessions did little to change their papers. Although we had dedicated two days to revision, the students' rough drafts looked nearly identical to their final drafts.

While my students saw little value in the feedback and revision process, experienced writers know that it is essential to direct our revision to areas that need additional attention so we are able to continue to grow our writing abilities.

HOW TO TALK ABOUT WRITING

In order for revision to be a more meaningful process, you must model how to talk about writing. It doesn't matter how much time you block out for peer editing or how many points you assign for revision in the rubric. Students will continue to struggle with revision until they learn how to have a conversation about writing with their peers.

When I think about growth-mindset feedback, I recall Gravity Goldberg's description of the different stances we take as teachers when we work with our students.[34] Rather than seeing our students through data and behaviors, Goldberg encourages teachers to take the stance of an admirer. Rather than noticing student deficits or what they need "fixed," we can approach our student's writing process through a lens of wonder, expectation, and admiration. Using an admirer's lens, we would frame our feedback in observations (I noticed that you started this paragraph with a question. Can you tell me more about why you chose that approach?), rather than critique (Don't start your paragraph with a rhetorical question).

By modeling this type of feedback language, you show your students that peer feedback should not just be correcting or "fixing" their classmate's writing. Instead, peer feedback starts with seeking to understand the writer's process, and then sharing your perspective as a reader. When I first began making these small changes in my feedback and modeling the language in front of my students, I watched their confidence in peer feedback increase dramatically. They were no longer anxious about "correcting" their friend's paper or even making it worse with "corrections" that were actually wrong. They felt much more comfortable asking questions, sharing their observations, and just talking about the writing.

Before your students begin to copyedit grammar or mechanics, move them into groups to read their writing aloud, ask questions, and listen to feedback from their group. Kelly Gallagher invites his students to participate in weekly writing groups, where each student reads their paper aloud and then receives specific feedback in the form of *bless* (positive comments), *address* (comments or questions on a particular section), or *press* (comments to make the paper stronger).[35] In the Action Steps on page 73, I share my routine for training students to participate in peer response groups. After a decade of trial and error, these steps have greatly increased the value of peer feedback in my writing classroom.

Ideally, your students will also come to see that *giving* feedback is often just as beneficial to their growth as receiving feedback from others. By analyzing the effectiveness of someone else's text and providing clear suggestions and feedback, they develop a stronger objectivity about their own work. The more adept they become at critically evaluating each other's writing, the more they come to recognize areas for revision in their own writing.

When we see our students working hard, we naturally want to offer feedback that will encourage and energize them for the steps ahead. However, Dweck advises teachers and parents to be aware of the implicit-mindset messages communicated through the language of our praise. When our feedback celebrates the writer's abilities (You're such a gifted writer! You're so good at this!), we send the message that success is tied to an inherent, inborn quality or talent. Dweck and Claudia Mueller's research showed that when students are praised for their ability, they resisted challenge and even began to cheat, as the burden of being "smart" became their sole focus.[36] Rather than encouraging them, the ability-praise filled them with fear and doubt.

Instead of ability-praise, offer feedback that acknowledges the successful actions within the process: the student's effort, flexibility, practice, problem-solving strategies, and willingness to seek help when needed. This process praise (Your hard work on this writing really paid off!) sends the message that success is due to the student's effort and the strategies they used, both of which they can control. According to Dweck and Mueller, the students praised for their effort came to understand that making mistakes was part of working hard and trying new things, rather than a reflection of their ability. Even more, praising their efforts actually increased their overall achievement.

By providing meaningful teacher feedback to all of your students, you teach writers to develop a writing process that anticipates and relies on revision for continued growth.

ACTION STEPS

1. PROVIDE STUDENTS WITH THE TRAINING TO PARTICIPATE IN MEANINGFUL PEER RESPONSE

To give your students feedback from a variety of perspectives, spend at least one day training them to talk about writing with each other, and then provide instructions for their response group assignment.

- In my classes, I assign three readings prior to the training: "Responding—Really Responding—to Other Students' Writing," by Richard Straub; "The Maker's Eye: Revising Your Own Manuscripts," by Don Murray; and "Workshop Is Not for You," by Jeremiah Chamberlin. After the students read the three articles, they respond to these questions:

  » What are your experiences with responding to other students' writing? Have you done so in other classes? How helpful were the responses you received from other students? Did you feel confident in offering your feedback to another writer? What have you felt your role was when responding to other students' writing? How do your experiences sound the same or different from Straub's suggestions? What advice did you find helpful?

» Straub shows you a responder—Jeremy—and the comments he wrote on Todd's paper. Do you agree with Straub's analysis of Jeremy's comments? What three or four additional things would you tell Todd about his paper?

» Don Murray explains the way professional writers use revision throughout the drafts. If you took Murray's advice for revision, how might it change your writing process?

» Chamberlin claims, "Workshop is not for you." What does he mean? Who is it for?

• Discuss previous experiences with revision. My students always related to Straub's article, feeling similar frustrations with peer-editing assignments.

• In order to show them the difference between "fix-it" feedback and response-group feedback, share videos of students working in response groups. You can find short videos of model response groups on YouTube, or record a group of your own students or colleagues. Pause the video to highlight moments when the students are discussing the writing as observers, rather than just telling a peer what they should "fix."

• Finally, read aloud a sample piece of your own writing, then ask the students to provide you with feedback. I read my early draft of "Underwater Smells" to the class and then asked them the following questions: Which section drew you in the most? What word choices were the most powerful? What areas were confusing? Could I cut out any words while still retaining the meaning? By considering these questions, students will practice their stance as an admirer of the writing, rather than the fixer. Since the questions do not focus on identifying errors (especially grammar and punctuation), the teenagers feel safe to offer their perspective.

EXAMPLE: "Underwater Smells"

I never knew there were smells underwater. The smells of fish, seaweed, dirt. The smells that follow you home and remain on your suit long after you laid it out in the sun to dry. The next time you wear it, it still smells the same. The bottom of the lake smell.

I remember one particularly cold swim I took with Andy and the other boys. We were playing submarine, and I was the torpedo. I was sent behind the buoy with Andy, and we counted while waiting for the other submarines to start their missions.

"Ten…nine…eight…seven…six…five…"

Andy detected the enemy on the shore side of the dock. "Fire!" he instructed, and I drew in air and dove under the water. But my ponytail caught on the underside of the dock as I fired, and, although my hair was long, it wasn't long enough for me to see the problem and untangle it, or to surface for a breath. I wanted to scream, to fight, to go back in time and ignore my inner tomboy. To instead make the choice to go to town flaunting denim skirts and blue eye-shadow with the rest of the girls, *to breathe.*

I couldn't think. My lungs burned. Not the kind of burn when you take your toast out of the toaster and accidentally graze a knuckle on the side, but the kind of burning when the wind suddenly changes directions at a bonfire and your lungs and eyes scream for clean air.

The panic of suffocation is profound. I sunk my fingernails into the algae on the underside of the dock. I inhaled it. I pleaded with it.

Finally, Andy and the other boys grabbed me and pulled me out. The dock kept a piece of my scalp as a souvenir.

But, by then I had drowned, so my bald spot was rather insignificant.

My mother never suggested covering my bald spot at my open casket funeral, as I would have expected her to do. But she did whisper across the pillow to my father, on the day they lowered me into the ground, that my hair smelled like the bottom of the lake.

- Reproducible #4: Response Groups Assignment (page 148) guides students in their time in response groups. It includes both the directions for the class time conversation and the letters that they will compose as homework. I review the assignment on the training day, so they can go right into their response groups (usually three or four students per fifty-five minutes) during the next class period. During this time, I rotate around the room and hallway space, sitting in for five to ten minutes with each response group.

2. SHARE THE REVISION OF SUCCESSFUL WRITERS

Another way to emphasize the importance of feedback is to share the revision process of professional writers.

One of America's best writing teachers, Don Murray, describes his meticulous revision process in a short essay, "The Maker's Eye," which starts by emphasizing the role of revision: "When professional writers complete their first draft, they usually feel they are at the start of the writing process."[37] In *Bird by Bird*, best-selling author Anne Lamott argues for the necessity of "the down draft—you just get it down."[38] Her revision process then moves her to the second draft, which is "the up draft—you fix it up. You try to say what you have to say more accurately." Finally, she works on the third draft, which is "the dental draft, where you check every tooth, to see if it's loose or cramped or decayed, or even, God help us, healthy."[39]

These examples help students see that the best possible writing requires reader feedback and ongoing revision. Professional writers not only expect a lot of revision, but also find it necessary for success!

By teaching students about the writing process of contemporary writers, you emphasize the point that even the world's best writers don't write it "right" the first time! Successful writers still need *a lot* of feedback and spend much of their time in the revision stage. Here are some examples I have used:

- On his blog, author Patrick Rothfuss was asked about his revising process for *The Kingkiller Chronicle* series, which is currently being adapted for film and television by Lin-Manuel Miranda, who wrote the script and music for *Hamilton*.[40] The inquiry came from James, a college student, who was wondering what takes Rothfuss so long to revise, as James saw his own process for writing papers as quite simple: "write, spell check, print, and then hand them in." In response, Rothfuss shared lengthy notes that detail exactly what he did in the course of one night's revision. His revision work includes twenty-six separate revision steps, ranging from changes to content ("Invented several new religious terms") to analyzing specific word choice ("Looked at my use of the word "vague" to see if I've been using it too much"). His revision notes also include a section that demonstrates his own trial and error ("Moved chapter. Read section of the book with new chapter order. Moved chapter back to where it was before."). Rather than the sequential steps of James's writing process, Rothfuss's notes show that for an expert writer, the flow of revision is often recursive as we go forward, backward, over there, and back again.

- J. K. Rowling, a name most students will quickly recognize, shared another great example of revision on her website, in an image titled "Revision of the plan of 'Order of the Phoenix.'" Her caption read: "Part of the umpteenth revision of the plan of 'Order of the Phoenix.' Some of the Chapter Names changed and there are a few ideas that didn't make the final draft."[41]

Invite students to look at all the "messiness" in her planning, noticing all of the decisions, changes, and new thoughts that are part of the writing process!

- Share your own experiences with feedback and revision. When I was in graduate school, I frequently brought in drafts of my dissertation to show my writing students, pages covered in comments from my committee and classmates. I showed other writings of mine that were currently in the revising process, pointing out the changes I was making based on the feedback from my weekly writing group. If I were in the classroom right now, I would share the numerous drafts of this book and comments from my editor. These personal examples reinforce the main point: good writers need feedback and revision to keep growing their skills!

3. USE PRAISE LANGUAGE TO HIGHLIGHT STUDENT EFFORT AND GROWTH

Teacher feedback not only communicates information, but what you value in learning. You can modify or add process praise into your writing feedback, making sure you send positive-mindset messages when you notice your students working hard!

Ability vs. Process Praise	
ABILITY PRAISE	PROCESS PRAISE
You come up with ideas so easily!	I like how you used a lot of different brainstorming strategies to generate these new ideas.
You're such a good writer!	I have seen so much growth in your writing this semester!
What a brilliant storyteller!	I love how you added a lot of sensory details to make your story even more engaging.
Writing is so natural for you!	I have noticed your passion for writing. Let's see how we can challenge you!
You have been given a gift for writing.	I can tell you are paying extra attention to the importance of great word choice.
You are the best writer in the class.	All of your hard work at revision really paid off!

CHAPTER 8

STRATEGY #5: OFFER FORMATIVE FEEDBACK DURING THE WRITING PROCESS

> **CENTRAL GROWTH-MINDSET BELIEF:** Giving feedback during the writing process provides an opportunity for students to use the feedback and grow their writing skills.

When writers receive feedback during their writing process and have the opportunity to use that feedback in revision, research shows they experience greater growth.[42] Rather than responding on finished drafts, give feedback throughout the drafting process, so students have time to utilize your questions and suggestions, make mistakes, try new techniques, and experiment with their writing. When you provide substantive feedback and create time for revision, your students will know that you value the growth and development in their thinking and writing.

While teacher feedback is essential for developing writers, it is only useful to the extent that students have the chance to apply it. Comments on final drafts or summative assessments do little to improve student writing. These comments only receive a passing glance as the student scans for a grade and then shoves the paper into a folder or a trash can. Once the writing has reached the point of grading, the student's writing process is over. Our summative comments are often useless. Although we might wish that students could somehow store our feedback and be able to recall it the next time they sit down to start a new piece, the truth is that they do not. Therefore, it is unfair to only offer students detailed feedback when we grade their work. By then it is too late.

Instead, I give my students the opportunity to use my feedback while the writing is being drafted. This is when they are open to learning and less defensive, and they have time to apply my instruction. While the students are writing, you can offer process feedback through one-on-one conferences or marginal and terminal comments on individual drafts. Using growth-oriented feedback language will motivate your students to work hard and grow as writers during the stage of revision. However, in order to provide timely feedback, you will need to regularly read drafts, assess your students' needs, and make time for individual writing conferences.

FEEDBACK LANGUAGE IN WRITING CONFERENCES

In individual conferences, teacher feedback can help facilitate greater growth in student thinking about the writing process. Five years ago, I participated in a workshop where I learned a new feedback language based on a nonjudgmental process of cognitive coaching, or mediation, with the goal of enhancing the writer's resourcefulness and autonomy. In this process, the teacher serves as a mediator of thinking, using a series of guided questions to help the student analyze their writing process and develop his or her own problem-solving strategies.

The language of cognitive coaching dramatically shifted my feedback language to communicate my values and beliefs about students and about writing. Even if we are not stating our beliefs directly, our coaching language can show students our commitment to greater growth. To encourage your students to talk more, for example, resist the urge to jump in with your corrections as soon as a student takes a breath. Through coaching feedback, we show respect for the student's autonomy as the writer and encourage them to articulate their thoughts using higher-order thinking skills of analysis, evaluation, and synthesis. Rather than just telling students what to "correct," engage them in critical thinking and problem-solving, so that they develop transferable skills that will be usable in many different situations.

In a writing conference, cognitive coaching questions ask students to do the following:

- specify indicators of success (What parts of your writing are you proud of? What is working well?)

- accurately self-assess their own abilities and areas of growth (What sections are you still struggling in? What sentences are still frustrating you?)

- make decisions about which strategies to use in response (What do you plan to do next? What will you do if you run out of ideas? What have you done to be successful in the past? What resources would be the most helpful?)

ACTION STEPS

1. OFFER PROCESS FEEDBACK THROUGH MARGINAL COMMENTS

While reading through new writing, incorporate growth-oriented feedback in your marginal comments, making notes about the areas you enjoy, the questions you have, and the places you feel confused. By offering feedback as a reader or an admirer, you leave it to the writer to make decisions about revision. For example, an admirer might state,

"I feel confused by these two sentences. Are you trying to say your dog was lost or that you were just worried about her?" It is up to the writer how they will rewrite that section to clear up any misunderstandings.

Rather than providing the advice, ideas, or solutions, this process invites students to do the heavy lifting and make their own decisions during the writing process. Acting as a sounding board, a skilled mediator will also help the student become more self-directed in their learning. Through coaching, students are able to develop trust in and articulate their own ideas. At the same time, you demonstrate your faith in the student's capacity for continued growth and higher achievement.

Address specific words, sentences, and paragraphs in your marginal comments with the goal of helping the student develop as a writer. Through praise, suggestions, or questions, call attention to the writer's strengths and the areas for growth that you notice in the writing. Marginal comments may also deal with larger issues of organization, tone, argument, and style. Overall, growth-oriented marginal comments should do the following:

- Use specific language in phrases or questions

- Adopt a tone of a supportive coach and interested reader

- Be careful not to freeze or overwhelm the student with excessive use

- Balance advice and criticism with praise

- Be specific in the concern and give direction for revision. Teacher shorthand (e.g., wc, awk, or frag) can be very confusing to students. (Instead of using "awk," say "I stumbled here.")

Marginal Comment as Praise: Great sentence! It nicely wraps up your thought and transitions into your next idea.

Marginal Comment as Revision Suggestion: How about a stronger verb to make this sentence more powerful? Look for other weak verbs (got, went, took, said, did) that you can turn into stronger, more precise verbs. I often use a thesaurus to find better verbs!

2. OFFER PROCESS FEEDBACK THROUGH TERMINAL COMMENTS

At the end of the writing, provide terminal or summary comments. It is important to begin these overall impressions by highlighting the writer's strengths. Writing is deeply personal, and you need to validate the good that you find, even if it is just a great topic choice. Then you can switch over to your teacher voice in an effort to provide students with clear direction and next steps.

According to *The St. Martin's Guide to Teaching Writing*, terminal comments "must do a great deal in a short space: they must document the strengths and weaknesses of an essay, let the student know whether she responded well to your assignment, help create a psychological environment in which the student is willing to revise or write again, encourage and discourage specific writing behaviors, and set specific goals that you think the student can meet."[43] Growth-oriented terminal comments do the following:

- Balance praise and areas for growth

- Address next steps or focus areas for revision

- Use thoughtful language to create a safe, open tone (see Strategy 7: Building Trust and Community for further discussion)

- Center on the writing, rather than the student ("Each of your central points needs an additional example" vs. "You need better examples")

- Consider the student's goals and suggest future goals

Terminal Comment as Praise: Great work! I can see you have put a lot of hard work into your paper after our first conference. Your first and second points are much stronger since you added the additional examples from your new source.

Terminal Comment as Revision Suggestion: In order to make sure your reader is convinced of your thesis, I think we still need to make the last point stronger. Could you find a personal story or quote from an expert and explain how it supports your point? You already have great statistics, but I think we could add additional appeals of ethos and/or pathos. If you can develop that last point a bit more, I think it will make your entire argument more effective.

In order to grow as writers, we all need to listen to critique, as it helps us identify what isn't working in our writing. Yet constructive feedback can feel hurtful at times, especially to sensitive student writers. To help manage these emotions, encourage students to perceive critique as valuable information or data, rather than an indication of poor writing skills. I remind my students that when a reader asks a clarifying question, makes note of a confusing section, or requests more evidence, they are merely pointing out a place that I can strengthen my current draft. For whatever reason, that section seems "off" to them. The student does not necessarily need to alter the draft in the way that the reader recommends, for they are the writer, but they do need to consider the reader's feedback in their revision. By framing the critique as information, rather than an indicator of their inability to write well, students will feel less defensive or hurt. Once they no longer view critique as a personal attack, they welcome the critique as data to help make their writing stronger.

3. ENGAGE STUDENTS IN COGNITIVE COACHING

Use a cognitive coaching model during the writing process, in which the feedback language encourages the student's self-directedness and development of cognitive complexity. These comments draw to the consciousness of the students, providing greater awareness for the choices they have made and the strategies they will use in the future.

EXAMPLE: Cognitive Coaching Questions for Writing Feedback

- What are you doing as a writer today?
- What was your thinking about _____?
- What were some of the criteria you used when selecting _____?
- How did you make decisions about _____?
- What are you hoping to accomplish in _____?
- What is your goal in this writing? How might you know when you have reached it?
- In what sequence might you approach _____?
- How long are you anticipating _____ will take?
- What might you need to do to be best prepared for _____?
- What might be some strategies you have used before that were effective in _____?
- What kind of help might be useful to you with _____?
- How might some of your peers support you with _____?
- How does _____ compare to how you planned it?
- Which resources seemed most useful when working on _____?
- What are some of the things you did to make _____ go so well?
- What are some of the resources you could have utilized but did not?
- How do you think your readers received your writing?
- Why is _____ important to you?
- What are some of the things you'd like to keep in mind when _____?
- What are some of your options when _____?
- What are you doing to try to make _____ your best?
- What ideas did you take from our previous conferences?

- How is _____ similar to something you've written before? How is it different?

- How will you celebrate your success in _____?

4. MANAGE YOUR TIME FOR ONGOING, TIMELY FEEDBACK

Providing ongoing process feedback for all students sounds intimidating because it requires the one thing all teachers lack: time. Even if you are sacrificing all of your evenings and Sunday afternoons, you may still struggle to manage the constant stack of student papers. Yet you must offer timely feedback on student writing. Feedback given immediately, or as soon as possible, significantly improves performance, and students need feedback throughout their writing process in specific, writer-centered, digestible ways.

In order to provide students with consistent feedback, you can adopt time-saving strategies. Luckily, a number of highly skilled veteran teachers have shared tips and tricks. Here are a few of my favorites:

- Jim Burke provides a useful approach for written feedback by noting significant errors occurring throughout a student's piece.[44] Rather than commenting on every error, he notes the issue at the top of the paper for easy reference and then follows up in an in-class conference. For example, he recognizes that the paper lacks a clear subject in most sentences, so he would underline or highlight numerous examples. He would then jot "clear subjects" on the top of the paper. These notes provide direction for the in-class writing conference and save him time when giving feedback on student drafts.

- In *Write Beside Them*, Penny Kittle details time and classroom management strategies that allow for in-class conferences.[45] She forms student response groups, training small groups of three writers to give meaningful feedback to one another (see my response group process outlined in Strategy #4: Provide Equitable

Feedback). These additional readers offer the writer a broader perspective on their piece and also ensure that the students read and reread their writing many more times. By training students to be effective responders, teachers no longer carry the entire feedback load on their own.

- In order to build in more time for direct feedback during writing workshop, Leah Mermelstein recommends that we create classroom environments that encourage self-regulation.[46] Build in resources to help keep students engaged when working independently and to help solve the inevitable problems that arise during the writing process. In classroom environments that targeted self-directed learning, Mermelstein found these common features:

  » Process and craft charts displayed on walls (For example, "What Can You Do When You Think You Are Finished?")
  » Mentor texts available for students
  » Writing supplies organized and available for student use
  » Student writing samples available for students

According to Mermelstein, "The setup of your classrooms can help kids become more resourceful, more independent, more persistent, more resilient, and better able to self-regulate their learning."

- Kelly Gallagher, one of my favorite writing teachers, stresses the need for feedback, while also realizing the realistic time constraints.[47] In order to regularly assess his students' understanding, he includes daily writing and reading conferences in every classroom. In his efforts to meet with as many students as often as possible, he has found ways to shorten and streamline his conferences by watching master teachers engage in and move through student conferences, such as Nancie Atwell in *Writing in the Middle*. Penny Kittle also models how to conduct student conferences in the *Write Beside Them* companion DVD.[48]

- *Papers, Papers, Papers* by Carol Jago is an entire book of great tips for saving time and managing your workload.[49] Jago's classroom practices that follow have helped me focus my feedback:

  » Be selective about what you read. In order to survive the paper load, Jago reads and responds to every student essay, but not much else that students write. All other types of writing (e.g., writing notebooks, class exercises, reading answers) are shared in other ways, like classroom discussions or pair-share.

  » Assign alternative assignments. Rather than assigning a five-page essay in every unit, use other genre forms that will still assess the standards but cut down on the stack of reading. Students can still move through the process of draft-feedback-revise while working on a writing assignment in a different genre. For example, rather than a character analysis essay, the same skills could be demonstrated through a poetic verse, persuasive letter, or diary entry.

  » Address common issues as a group. When reading through student papers, Jago keeps track of recurring errors and pulls specific examples from the paper pile for future mini-lessons. When handing back papers, she spends ten to twenty minutes addressing common errors and answering questions with the entire class.

  » One of my favorite Jago tips is the concept of grading parties! Schedule an evening or weekend retreat with other writing teachers and dedicate portions of your time together to grading. Not only does this time provide a sense of camaraderie, but you also have colleagues to share ideas and offer their opinions. These professional learning communities can be a great way to measure validity in your grading practices and mentor early career teachers.

CHAPTER 9

STRATEGY #6: SHARE THE IMPORTANCE OF SELF-TALK

> **CENTRAL GROWTH-MINDSET BELIEF:** Self-talk is critical for managing mindsets and increasing student agency.

Encouraging positive self-talk is another important way to foster growth mindsets while working with student writers. If you have spent any amount of time in a writing classroom, you have most likely heard students make self-defeating announcements: "I cannot write," "I'll never be a good writer," or "My writing is terrible."

Erin, one of the strongest writers in my class, regularly referred to her writing as "garbage" or "trash" during our individual conferences, despite the high grades she continued to receive on her essays. Other types of negative self-talk, such as "This assignment is really hard," or "I'm not going to be able to write enough," reflects low writing efficacy in our students and can stem from fixed-mindset beliefs. Negative self-talk can become toxic to a student's motivation, confidence, and the act of writing itself; however, you can help students gain awareness and even alter the mindset voices influencing their feelings about writing.

You can start combating negative self-talk by educating students about the voices inside of their head. These internal voices, which we call self-talk, can be positive and motivate our students, or they can be negative and hold them back from achieving their goals. Self-talk has the power to influence thoughts, affect confidence, and compel behaviors. In addition, the fixed- and growth-mindset beliefs, which we all possess, come alive through this internal dialogue running through our heads. Both types of mindsets can compete for control of our self-talk, especially when we face setbacks and challenges, and the voices we allow in our heads can impact our successes or failures.

The danger in negative self-talk is that it reinforces the *victimicity* or passivity present in fixed-mindset beliefs, and ultimately determines the writers our students will become.[50] When a student says to themself, "I'll never be able to do this assignment," they are interpreting their struggle as an indication of low or absent ability. The student believes they have no agency in the situation, as their ability level is already predetermined. These beliefs then impact the student's response, which often results in unproductive behaviors such as avoidance, defiance, or giving up all together in order to save face. Of course, without any continued effort, the student will demonstrate little growth or achievement. As a result, the initial self-talk becomes a self-fulfilling prophecy.

Conversely, students become more strategic and successful writers when they engage in positive self-talk. We can help our students develop an internal dialogue that helps them grow by building and rebuilding constructive self-talk. Teacher researchers Kristine Mraz and Christine Hertz point out that students' brains are still building the neural pathways around their most common thought processes, which clearly shows the importance of the self-talk our students are using the most.[51] If you can help students recognize and change their patterns of thought, you can help them construct new neural pathways, which will lead them to engage in productive and positive self-talk. In order to deconstruct the negative thought processes and create more positive pathways, your students must reflect on their thoughts through both writing activities and open discussion.

Since words have great power over our students' beliefs about themselves as writers, self-talk is critical to controlling mindsets. When students start to identify their thoughts about writing, they can determine which mindset is controlling their internal voices and work to reframe them when necessary. They must be able to tell the difference between the two mindset beliefs, so they can respond when fixed-minded self-talk tries to sabotage their efforts.

You can model positive self-talk when you talk about experiences in which you have encountered a challenge or setback. While telling a story, embed positive phrases to demonstrate growth-minded thinking. For example, I often share my experience of writing a dissertation with my high school writers, even bringing in drafts that are covered in comments from my professors and other readers. I tell the students that while I initially felt discouraged by all of the feedback, I had to switch my thinking. Rather than saying "I'm never going to finish this paper," I reminded myself that "these comments will help me create a stronger argument." When you teach students to understand the ways their brains work and model how to think about our abilities, you give them the tools that they can use in their own continued reflections.

When students reframe fixed-mindset messages, they should also be aware of Carol Dweck's "yet" strategy. In her TED talk, Dweck explains how the little word *yet* can give us a lot of power, as it implies that success is still possible.[52] Just because we haven't reached a goal yet does not mean that we should give up or quit trying. When your students speak of their difficulties in terms of failure, which is perceived as definitive and final, you can encourage them to attach the words *yet* or *not yet* to their current struggle. This approach is especially important to emphasize in a writing classroom, where the act of writing is not a "one and done," but a process through which the writer continues to improve the piece they are working on. For example, when you hear a student say "I can't write a strong thesis," you can rephrase their comment as "I haven't written a strong thesis *yet*." The *yet* implies that the student will be able to succeed sometime in the future. This small change conveys the promise of better things ahead, as it reminds the student that they are still in the process of growing as writers. When students believe that they will, with effort and persistence, be successful, they are more likely to remain on a path of continued growth.

PRACTICING OPTIMISM

In addition, you can share with students the benefits of practicing positivity and optimism. Children are often willing to take chances and try new things but tend to lose their sense of optimism as they grow older. They become more cautious and pessimistic after they encounter failure, judgment, and disappointment. Many of our students have already become hesitant and anxious about writing, happy to just coast through five-paragraph essays or other formulaic writing assignments. When they do encounter setbacks or failure, they respond with pessimism and quickly turn to fixed-mindset thoughts, such as "I'm such a bad writer" or "I'll never be able to write a good story." They will likely blame others for their failure as well: "I just didn't get good feedback from my group," or "All of the topic choices were boring!" Clearly pessimism can quickly spiral into fixed-minded thinking about writing.

However, when you invite your students to practice optimism, you alter their initial reactions to difficult tasks. Rather than fear an unfamiliar or challenging writing assignment, they feel hopeful and are willing to give it their best shot. As growth-minded writers, they understand that even if they fail, they can bounce back and grow from that experience.

Similar to positive self-talk, you can teach optimism with continued practice and effort. When you invite students to be optimistic and hopeful, you encourage their curiosity and wonder, which builds their confidence to take risks and enjoy challenges. Optimism will benefit all your students, as it helps to build a growth-oriented mindset, open to new learning and confident in the ability to succeed.

ACTION STEPS

1. INVITE STUDENTS TO "TALK BACK" TO FIXED-MINDED THOUGHTS

Once students develop an awareness of the damage negative thoughts can cause, give them opportunities to practice "talking back" to their fixed-minded internal dialogue. The chart below gives examples of self-talk we may hear from our fixed writing mindsets. Ask students to "talk back" to the statements using growth-minded statements about writing. The first example shows how we can "talk back" to the fixed mindset statement by using Dweck's "yet" strategy. After responding to these fixed-mindset statements, students can take turns sharing their own negative self-talk, and invite a partner to talk back!

Example: Talk Back to Fixed-Mindset Thoughts	
FIXED-MINDSET THOUGHT	**TALK BACK!**
I can't think of anything to write. I might as well give up!	I can't think of anything to write yet! How about asking my teacher for some brainstorming strategies?
I can never get started writing.	I know the steps to start! I'll just try!
My papers are always horrible.	I may have made mistakes before, but I can learn and change!

See Reproducible #5: Talk Back to Fixed-Mindset Thoughts (page 151) for the complete chart.

2. PREPARE TO FACE MINDSET TRIGGERS

Help students identify and prepare for writing situations that trigger negative emotional reactions and fixed-mindset responses. When do student writers begin to feel anxious, frustrated, or hopeless during the writing process? A fixed-mindset trigger might occur in the writing classroom when they run into writer's block, receive negative feedback, or feel overwhelmed by a large writing assignment. Once your students notice these patterns, they can begin preparing themselves to deal with these triggers in the future.

Brock and Hundley recommend that teachers incorporate a mini-lesson to target students' mindset triggers.[53] Once the trigger is identified, the students can then create a plan where they will recognize the situation and respond with a growth-mindset approach, combating the feelings of failure and victimhood, and focusing instead on their own agency.

Help students to develop a plan for moving forward by identifying the specific circumstances, places, or people that trigger negative self-talk and feed their fixed mindsets. By planning and preparing to face the negative voices, students can seek out strategies to manage their mindsets.

EXAMPLE: Plan for Mindset Triggers

My mindset trigger is _____

The circumstances (places, people, situations) that usually trigger me are...

The negative self-talk statements I usually tell myself are...

This makes me feel...

When I face my mindset trigger from now on, I will use these positive statements...

My positive self-talk will help me feel...

Additional resources or strategies that can support me are...

---

3. FIGHT FEAR WITH OPTIMISM AFFIRMATIONS

Students can practice optimistic thinking through affirmations, in which they verbalize their value, ability, or potential for success in statements like "My ideas matter to others," or "I will do my best today." The affirmations may be written by you or the students, either about themselves or a peer. These affirmations might be read aloud or serve as a prompt for an optimism reflection, such as: "I will do my best today." When is a day that you genuinely felt like you tried your best? How did your day turn out?

During my visit to a small alternative school, the principal gathered all her students together in a large meeting room on the first morning. As each student entered the room, they selected one index card from a table and then stepped into a large circle of their peers. One by one, students read aloud from their cards, each one stating a positive affirmation to begin the day, such as "I will succeed today!" or "I am an important member of this community!"

I was inspired to see this principal prioritizing the affirmations for each of her students, many of whom had failed in another school setting, which established a learning environment of hope and optimism. Regardless of how each student felt when they entered school that morning, they adopt a growth mindset as they spoke the affirmations.

EXAMPLE: Optimism Affirmations

I know I can write this!

Challenges will help me grow.

I will succeed today.

My ideas are important to others.

I will reach my writing goal.

Even if I don't succeed at first, I will keep trying.

My voice has power to make positive change.

I am resilient.

I am a hard worker.

My teacher and classmates will help me when I struggle.

Even if I feel scared, I will try new things.

My revision efforts will pay off.

Today is a new day!

Failure does not define me.

Mistakes are opportunities for learning.

---

4. INCLUDE GRATITUDE AND OPTIMISM PROMPTS IN DAILY JOURNAL WRITING

Many teachers use journal writing as a key component of their daily classroom practices; journals offer a great space to practice positive self-talk. You can create mindset prompts to meet a specific goal, such as prewriting for an upcoming assignment, or to just increase writing fluency. A daily writing prompt can provide a good routine, as students enter class and immediately take out their journals to begin writing. As you create many different prompts to engage student writers, you may also include writing topics that evoke feelings of gratitude and optimism. For example, students could list items, experiences, or people they are grateful for or free-write about a specific event that illustrates gratitude or optimism. You can find additional growth-mindset journal prompts in my resource *180 Ready-to-Use Growth Mindset Prompts*.[54]

EXAMPLE: Gratitude Journal Prompts

What are different ways that you show your gratitude to others?

Name ten things you are grateful for: two things you taste, two things you hear, two things you smell, two things you touch, and two things you see.

Describe a teacher, coach, or mentor that you are grateful to have in your life. How have they impacted you in positive ways?

What are some items that you are grateful for but often take for granted?

Imagine you could create a new holiday to celebrate one person in your life that you love (for example: Grandpa Ross or Aunt Jill Appreciation Day). If you had unlimited resources, how would you spend the day celebrating?

CHAPTER 10

STRATEGY #7: BUILD TRUST AND COMMUNITY

> **CENTRAL GROWTH-MINDSET BELIEF:** When teachers build trust and community in a growth-mindset classroom, students feel comfortable taking writing risks and engaging in challenging tasks.

In order to foster a growth mindset in writers, we can introduce challenges and encourage all students to take risks in their writing. In Strategy #3, I discussed the importance of identifying next steps—areas in which all students can stretch themselves as writers, as well as experience greater engagement and growth in their writing process. These moments of appropriate challenge and risk-taking can strengthen a writer's confidence in their abilities, which can result in both growth-mindset gains and increased writing achievement.

When you design challenging, meaningful writing tasks, students may respond differently depending on their beliefs about writing. If they believe that effort can grow their writing ability, they often approach a challenge with enthusiasm and curiosity; they feel more confident trying things that aren't easy or comfortable because they know it's okay not to be successful on the first try. Although they might fail at first, they are willing to take a risk in order to stretch their current abilities and ultimately grow as writers.

In contrast, students with a fixed mindset may feel threatened by writing tasks that require them to stretch their current abilities or take risks. These writers will feel threatened by the challenge, afraid they will not succeed. They fear that failure will confirm to themselves (and everyone else) that they are, as they suspected, bad writers. In order to avoid looking stupid, they will often give up quickly.

In order to build a classroom culture that embraces challenge and risk-taking, you must first gain your students' trust by establishing a supportive writing environment. We have all felt discouraged and knocked down as writers, most likely by a bad grade or hurtful comments on a piece of meaningful writing. When our students have these experiences, they come to see the writing classroom as an unfriendly, chaotic, high-risk, punitive place. However, in a classroom where you support your students and they encourage one another, you establish an environment for transformation. All writers can feel safe and empowered, trusting you enough to take risks and embrace the challenge that will lead to growth. Here are some ways to gain student trust and build a nurturing writing environment:

Provide a low-stakes setting, where students are able to write without any penalty for failing or making mistakes. In order to offer a growth-mindset ethos, encourage risk-taking rather than correctness, and frame mistakes as valued learning opportunities. When your students take risks, they may struggle while they are learning. Reassure students that things won't always work out as they want on the first try, but they won't be penalized for failure. In a growth-mindset writing classroom, every day is an opportunity for growth!

Create time for students to celebrate and reflect on their writing growth. When you spend time celebrating, you reinforce that you truly value risk-taking. By stopping to notice their progress and taking a moment to feel accomplished, writers are more willing to stretch and grow. If you want them to develop into fearless, persistent, risky writers, then you have to make it crystal clear that you admire risk-taking.

Although you want to celebrate student writing, you do not want to sacrifice two or three class periods to celebrate or share challenges through individual presentations. Instead, you can ask students to share their favorite sentence or paragraph with the class (known as the *Quaker Share*), or select a few different students with each writing assignment. In the companion DVD to her book *Write Beside Them*, Penny Kittle models the *Symphony Share,* where she shows other writing teachers how to recognize a few great lines of student work during writing conferences.[55] Near the end of the period, she asks those students to share their lines with the class, a short act of celebration that not only encourages them, but may also provide inspiration to the other students as they continue drafting. At the end of the week, you might also ask a few students to share a challenge they faced and the lesson that they learned from it.

CONSIDER!

How do your students feel when they take a risk or attempt a new challenge? What can you do to encourage your students to step outside their comfort zones? How can you celebrate students when they do take risks and embrace challenges?

Creating the conditions for risk-taking requires a delicate balance of high expectations and responsive support. When you encourage students to take a chance, you must be aware that they will often feel stuck and frustrated. If you want them to step into that discomfort, they must trust that you will support them in their struggle and see value in their work. When your students are in the middle of messy, risky work, you can be ready to respond to their needs by having strategies and resources in place, offering guided practice, and scaffolding the writing tasks.

When you meet writing challenges with a supportive classroom and responsive teaching, they can provide the perfect opportunity for growth.

Your "next steps" feedback can urge the student to give more effort and set new goals, while communicating your confidence in their potential. For a teacher whom they truly trust, your students will be ready to dive into the next steps.

CONSIDER!
What questions can you ask your students to better understand who they are as writers? What are signs that a student is engaged in a piece they are writing?

ACTION STEPS

1. USE WRITER-CENTERED FEEDBACK TO BUILD TRUST

If you want your students to believe in themselves, you must communicate that you believe in them too. Affirming teacher feedback is key to influencing student beliefs about their writing ability. Your words are powerful! You want to acknowledge student strengths while using a tone of openness as you encourage them to try something new. In a nurturing environment, your feedback responds to both the mind and the heart of a writer, recognizing that writing is an act of vulnerability. Your conversations about writing should consider both the content of the writing and the heart of the writers.

If you want students to take writing risks and embrace challenge, your feedback must communicate your care for each writer. Unsure if you are using writer-centered feedback? Use this checklist:

Writer-Centered Feedback

When I provide writing feedback...

I consider the writing mindset and goals of this student.

I name the writer's strengths and suggest next steps for growth.

I use helpful, specific language, not just empty praise for the writer.

My tone is one of openness rather than judgment.

I respect the student as the writer of this piece.

I recognize that our cultural backgrounds may impact our roles as writer and reader.

The purpose is helping my students improve.

I am a source of encouragement and support for my writers.

2. INCORPORATE WRITING NOTEBOOKS INTO YOUR CLASSROOM ROUTINE

When school supplies are at their lowest price, I purchase a large supply of one-subject spiral notebooks for the new school year. On the first day of class, each student receives their own writing notebook. I stay organized by keeping all of the notebooks for each class in their own basket, and they remain in my classroom. Since writing notebooks are a space where my students engage in daily, ungraded writing practice, I need them to be in the room every day.

To maintain trust with your students, it is important to clarify whether the prompt is a public or private entry before the writing begins. If you are planning to ask the students to share their notebook writing, make sure that they are aware of that prior to the writing. Since students often record personal thoughts and experiences in their writing notebooks, we want to respect their privacy and allow them to decide which writing they share with others.

All notebook activities should have low stakes, allowing students to take risks with genres and ideas as they free-write to writing prompts, brainstorm for longer pieces of writing, or practice a new technique. To further build the trust of your students, spend time writing in your own notebook when they are writing during class time. When they share their ideas, share yours as well. This shows that you won't ask anything of them that you are not willing to do yourself, even if it requires your own vulnerability. Worried about keeping kids accountable or engaged without a grade? See Strategy #10 for alternatives to assessment.

Each time I ask my students to take out their writing notebooks, I review the expectations for free-writing:

- The only requirement is to keep writing! Don't worry about your spelling, grammar, or random ideas. Just let your words flow out of your brain and down through your pen onto your paper.

- Free-writing is never graded. As long as you keep writing, you will receive full points.

- If you run out of ideas, switch to a different topic, but don't stop writing!

- If a notebook entry is private, I will be the only person who will read your response. Your writing will stay confidential, unless you write that someone is hurting you, or you are planning to harm yourself or someone else. However, during "public writing" days, you will be asked to share some of your writing with a partner.

It is important to note that I do not read or respond to all of the writing notebook entries. Many years ago, I attended a conference where a speaker significantly changed my teaching practice with one remark. He said, "If you are reading everything your students are writing, then they are not writing enough." His words reassured me that daily writing could still be purposeful and engaging for students, even if I did not read or respond to every entry. From that point on, my students began writing for at least fifteen minutes every day, but I focused my time and energy on providing feedback for their working drafts. If I feel that some sort of grade is necessary for the writing notebooks, I skim the notebooks once a week and record a small number of participation points.

Without grades and feedback, I needed to find other ways to motivate my students to remain engaged in the writing notebook activities. The first and most effective way is to provide highly engaging prompts that incorporate topics they value and want to discuss. Some of those are funny or quirky, while others are complicated and thought-provoking. At times, I ask the students to write about their experiences, while other times they write about an issue at school, in their community, or even in pop culture.

A second way you can maintain student motivation is through offering choice. Similar to the first approach, this offers students the opportunity to write about topics that matter to them. I am not suggesting that you provide no direction at all (although I sometimes remove all restrictions for a "Free-Write Friday"), but offer a number of questions that relate to a central subject, like my example on "firsts" in the prompts below.

EXAMPLE: Writing Notebook Prompts

Choice Free-write: Write an account of one of your "firsts": your first date; your first serious argument with your parents; your first experience with physical violence or danger; your first extended stay away from home; your first encounter with someone whose culture was very different from your own; your first experience with serious illness or death of a close friend or relative; your first day of school; your first broken heart, etc.

Quick Daily Free-write: What is dinnertime like in your house? How many times a week do you eat with your family? What activities and obligations make it difficult to eat together as a family? What is the value of a family to you?

Narrative Essay Prewriting Free-write: List fifteen memorable moments from your life. These might be important events (deaths, births, weddings, graduations) or everyday moments (meeting your best friend, a family road trip, or getting a new pet). Then choose one of those moments and describe the experience.

> **Argumentative Free-write:** After we finish reading "Teenage Wasteland," write one page explaining who you think is responsible for Donny's downfall. Make sure you include many specific details from the story. We will use these ideas to begin preparing for our classroom debate.

3. CREATE SAFE SPACES FOR PEER RESPONSE GROUPS

Students must trust that you will ensure safe spaces for peer response. Sharing one's writing is a vulnerable act, and we must train students to show empathy, respect, and kindness when giving supportive feedback to each other.

One way that I establish safe spaces is by working with students to create a list of group norms for our response groups. Establishing norms in your classroom will identify the acceptable behaviors that will support a meaningful discussion about writing. Additionally, the norms help maintain a safe space where writers feel supported, rather than judged or attacked.

You can start by handing out five Post-its to each student. Then ask them to jot down five behaviors that they would like to see in their writing group. As students record their ideas, pick up the Post-its and add them to your whiteboard, grouping similar ideas together. After the students spend time discussing the options in their small groups, work as a class to select norms that everyone can agree on and abide by. A student volunteer can record your norms on a large piece of paper, which stays clearly displayed in the room. Prior to each response group time, spend some time reviewing the expectations the class established with your group norms.

EXAMPLE: 10th Grade English Group Norms

Group Norms Contract

As a member of our group, I commit to...

✔ Participating by sharing my writing and giving feedback

✔ Listening closely when someone is reading. No interrupting!

✔ Using "I" rather than "You" when giving feedback, so no one feels attacked or defensive

✔ Staying focused on the writing! My phone will be put away during group time.

✔ Making sure all writers get equal time to share

✔ Balancing the amount of praise and suggestions

✔ RESPECTING the writer's experience and opinion even if it's different from mine

Signed _____

4. OFFER STUDENTS CHOICE IN WRITING TOPICS

Since my students write in their notebooks each day, I must allow them choice about their topics for a number of reasons. They show greater engagement, take ownership, and have an easier time generating ideas. As they spend time writing about their interests, experiences, and perspectives, I learn the unique personality of each of my students and together, we form meaningful relationships over the course of the semester.

When you build in opportunities for choice, students have agency to pursue their own interests and passions. This creates trust-filled classrooms, where students are motivated and empowered to explore new ideas while still meeting your expectations for an activity or assignment. Moreover, providing choice is a natural way to differentiate the requirements, providing a "next steps" challenge for each one of your students. If you focus on the skill at the heart of a standard, it is appropriate to offer students choice while still meeting your learning targets and assessing for mastery.

- Reproducible #6: Verse Novel Project (page 153) provides an example of a final assessment that offers a wide variety of ways for students to demonstrate their mastery for a unit on verse novels.

Example: Variations Allowing for Choice

STANDARD

The student will be able to determine a theme or central idea of a text and how it is conveyed through particular details. (CCSS.ELA-Literacy.RL.6.2)

ELEMENT OF CHOICE	EXAMPLE
After reading the novel I have selected for the class, students are allowed to choose the *genre* of their written analysis of a central theme. I offer a list of possible choices and the specific requirements for each, including a children's book, fashion designs, collection of journal entries, Spotify playlist, Pinterest board, or graphic novel.	Kevin loves music, so the option of a Spotify playlist jumps out. After brainstorming a few possible lists, he focuses on the theme "fate" (love just seemed too easy!). He spends hours selecting just the right songs that really show the struggle between fate and our own choices. He uses a computer program to design a Spotify song list. He hands in the image alongside a typed paper, in which he has analyzed the lyrics to each of his song selections and argued its relevance to the scenes and characters from the novel.

STANDARD

The student will be able to conduct a short research project that uses several sources to build knowledge through investigation of different aspects of a topic. (CCSS.ELA-Literacy.W.5.7)

○ ELEMENT OF CHOICE	EXAMPLE
My students can meet these learning targets using most any topic, so I structure this assignment like a Passion Project or Genius Hour. They can use their time to learn more about a topic that interests them.	Hannah loves dogs and is interested in creating a dog park in her neighborhood. She researches this topic by speaking with local experts, reading city ordinances, and pouring through dog park designs. At the end of the unit, she becomes the teacher, sharing her expertise and passion with her peers.

STANDARD

The student will be able to write a narrative to develop real or imagined experiences or events using effective technique, relevant descriptive details, and well-structured event sequences. (CCSS.ELA-Literacy.W.8.3)

ELEMENT OF CHOICE	EXAMPLE
For this learning target, I offer my students three different options. I want them to have choice, but I also want them to select events that have enough significance to make for a good narrative. Notice how each of the options still offers considerable choice, but with clear direction: (1) Describe an experience in which you were an outsider, (2) Describe a situation that you believe moved you out of childhood, (3) Explore an early experience with literacy (positive or negative) and how that moment impacts the reader or writer that you are today.	Shea selected the first option, writing the narrative story of her first day in America. She describes the confusion and isolation as she recounts her experience as an exchange student entering the unfamiliar world of Nashville, Tennessee. Although this challenge was difficult at times, she clearly shows how it made her a stronger and more independent young woman.

CHAPTER 11

STRATEGY #8: RECOGNIZE STRUGGLE AS NECESSARY FOR GROWTH

CENTRAL GROWTH-MINDSET BELIEF: When teachers normalize struggle within the writing process, students are able to navigate negative emotions and see the benefit for their continued growth.

Responding to failure, frustrations, and fear is central to our process as writers. At the same time, our reactions to these challenges are essential for our growth-mindset development. Since writing is neither natural nor easy, we can be certain that even successful writers encounter a great deal of failure and must remain resilient if they are to achieve their goals. In order for your students to overcome the obstacles in their writing process, they must also have opportunities to face challenges, struggle, and learn from those experiences.

When writing teachers encourage their students to try new approaches or take writing risks, they may meet resistance, as many students feel a great deal of fear about damaging their grades or looking stupid, and this fear works against their growth in the writing process. I can recall many times when I was excited to introduce a new authentic writing assignment to my students, but I ended up feeling disappointed with their lackluster responses. However, I now recognize that their hesitancy to move past traditional five-paragraph essays came from fear and insecurity about their own abilities. Although my new writing assignment may have been more engaging, it was unfamiliar, and the students worried about embarrassing themselves and falling short of my expectations. In order to reduce the frustration, struggle, and feelings of threat, my students just wanted to know how to please the teacher without putting forth too much extra effort. In addition, they wanted to succeed quickly, as they also interpret speed as an indicator of their ability.

NORMALIZING STRUGGLE

If teachers can normalize struggle within the writing process, students may be able to recognize discomfort as a necessary part of growth. For example, we often teach the writing process as a series of linear steps: brainstorm—rough draft—revise—edit—publish. However, authentic writing is usually much more fluid and complex for experienced writers, as they explore the ways that don't work in order to find the ways that do. They may jump from drafting back to brainstorming, then to more drafting and revision. Sometimes writers begin with drafting or freewriting, while other times we revise and edit at the same time. We may cut out several paragraphs while editing, and then search for new research just days before publishing. Rather than a sequence of steps forward, writing is a recursive process that requires persistence and tenacity.

Writing classrooms should make space for failure, reframing the struggle as something *good* writers work through, rather than an indicator of inadequacy or stupidity. As Anne Lamott says, good writers often start with "really, really shitty first drafts."[56] We do not want students to wallow alone in their frustrations about writing, yet we want them to struggle through just enough challenge in their writing to meet with success.

ACTION STEPS

1. SUGGEST STRATEGIES FOR STRUGGLING STUDENTS

When students struggle in their writing, you have the opportunity to step in and coach them through it. Rather than just pointing out mistakes, offer strategies for them to deploy. After they work through their issue, ask them to reflect on the lesson they learned or how that challenge helped them grow as a writer.

In a classroom where students believe that they can continue to grow as writers with additional effort and support, there are many possible paths to success. If one way does not work at first, they can adapt and try a different approach. We can help facilitate this perspective by encouraging students to use different strategies when they run into frustrations.

During a writing workshop session, you will likely notice some of your student writers feeling frustrated. Someone has run out of ideas for a particular topic and stares blankly at the screen. Across the room, someone else is muttering under their breath because they cannot figure out APA citation. Rather than immediately offering suggestions or answers to each of the students, how can you help them learn new strategies as a result of their struggle? The current approach does not seem to be working, so what can they try next? It is so important that we coach our students to adapt as they work through writing struggles, reminding them that when we work hard to get through our challenges, that is often when the deeper learning occurs.

The following example includes my observations from Mr. J.'s writing classroom as he provides meaningful feedback to his students.

> ## EXAMPLE: Classroom Snapshot
>
> As students spent time testing out their ideas, Mr. J. walked around offering feedback by asking questions to coach students through their cognitive processing: "Have you tried…?" "What if you…?" He encourages the teens to select a comfortable workspace and take "brain breaks" when necessary.
>
> A few students listen to headphones, while others remain silent. Mr. J helps students by offering strategies when they became stuck. When a boy complains that he can't think of anything more to write, Mr. J. encourages him to free-write in his writing notebook or create a list of questions a reader might ask. When another student asks about source citation, Mr. J. shares a couple of websites that model the various formats. After the girl two seats back complains that there are too many sources for her research topic, Mr. J. shows a small group of students how to filter the database sources by date, language, or topic.
>
> Through his feedback, Mr. J. fosters growth-mindset thinking by expecting his students will run into setbacks and providing resources and strategies to meet these challenges.

2. INCORPORATE STORIES FROM "FAMOUS FAILURES"

Celebrity stories can be a powerful way to show students how hard work and struggle yield great success! Storytelling "Famous Failures" emphasizes that success rarely comes quickly or on the first try; instead, mastery often emerges after decades of dedicated practice and repeated mistakes. Students may believe that their favorite athlete, inventor, or performer was just born great, with natural talents or gifts; however, they will be surprised to see that the greatest successes require an incredible amount of effort, grit, and persistence.

Share the stories of writers who showed persistence when faced with adversity or failure. Students can learn how Malcolm X used his time in prison to improve his reading and writing skills, or they can view J. K.

Rowling's rejection letters on Twitter.[57] Victor Villanueva, Sherman Alexie, Maya Angelou, Elaine Richardson, Nas, and many others faced obstacles caused by socioeconomic and racial inequality, yet their passion and love for learning led to great success and literary influence.[58]

Share videos featuring obstacles successful celebrities have faced, and then engage students in a discussion about the mindset or beliefs about abilities that they noticed in the video. For example, you can access videos like "Michael Jordan's 'Failure' Nike Commercial" or the story of Dick and Rick Hoyt.[59] To continue using these motivating messages, add "Famous Failure" quotes or images on sticky notes or bulletin boards around your classroom.[60]

Students can select a "Famous Failure" from the list below or choose another person at the top of their field. In a research assignment, the student would learn how the person developed their skills: the education they received, the mentors who helped along the way, the setbacks they encountered, and the factors that allowed them to persevere. Finally, students would learn about the figure's influence in their particular field. Following their research, the students can share the "Famous Failure" stories through their own poems, children's books, collages, raps, or videos.

EXAMPLE: List of "Famous Failures"

Steve Jobs	Michael Jordan	Walt Disney
Mark Zuckerberg	Mark Cuban	Oprah Winfrey
The Beatles	Ellen DeGeneres	Lady Gaga
J. K. Rowling	Winston Churchill	Thomas Edison
Eminem	Lucille Ball	Elvis Presley
Abraham Lincoln	Dr. Seuss	Tiffany Haddish
Kobe Bryant	Henry Ford	The Wright Brothers
Beyoncé Knowles-Carter		

3. LOOK FOR "FAILING FORWARD" STORIES

Use the power of storytelling to reframe failure in a growth-mindset classroom. Best-selling author John C. Maxwell uses the phrase "failing forward" to encourage his readers to recognize productive failure, in which mistakes and setbacks can be seen as valuable learning opportunities. As a classroom community, both teachers and students can share their stories of failure and mistakes, reflecting on the lessons they learned or the growth that followed those experiences.

Failure storytelling can help students make sense of their most painful moments while reframing the experience with powerful, positive self-talk. When you encourage your students to share their stories of failing forward, you create space for the belief that success is possible. While failure may still be painful for your students, it will no longer define who they are as writers.

Once I gained a firm understanding of growth-minded attitudes towards failure, I began to see examples everywhere! When I hear "failing forward" stories, I make sure to write myself a note or take a quick screenshot so I can share the example with my students. Students could search news articles or look into their family history for great "failing forward" stories to share with the class. I love to see the different ways that real people are "failing forward" all over the world.

EXAMPLE: Failing Forward Story

Fleeing from the Boko Haram terrorists at the age of seven, Nigerian refugee Tanitoluwa Adewumi was living in a homeless shelter in Manhattan when he joined the chess club at school. Three years later, he is one of the youngest people ever to become a national chess master. He credits failure as the key to his incredible success: "When you lose, you have made a mistake, and that can help you learn. I never lose. I learn."[61]

---

4. TAKE ADVANTAGE OF THE PASSITON. COM RESOURCES

The Foundation for a Better Life has launched the Pass It On campaign to communicate the benefits of a life lived with positive values. Their prints, commercials, and videos center on specific values—such as character, persistence, or passion—and define the words through an image of a hero and uplifting quote.[62] Many of the positive values, which have been shared through billboards across the country, perfectly align with the growth-minded characteristics.

The PassItOn.com offers posters and additional resources, as well as one really cool opportunity for students. After looking through the billboard examples, students can create their own billboards by choosing a value word, image, and text. This billboard activity would be a great final step for their "Famous Failures" story.

Example: Pass It On Billboards		
HERO	TEXT	VALUE
Abraham Lincoln	Failed, failed, failed. And then…	PERSISTENCE
Jackie Robinson	Here's to you, Mr. Robinson.	CHARACTER
Muhammad Ali	His biggest fight wasn't in the ring.	COURAGE
Babe Ruth	From orphanage to Hall of Fame.	DRIVE
Mia Hamm	Kicked her way to the top.	PASSION
Thomas Edison	On the 10,000th try, there was light.	OPTIMISM
Whoopi Goldberg	Overcame dyslexia.	HARD WORK

5. USE STORYTELLING TO SHARE EXPERIENCES OF SUCCESSFUL STRUGGLE

Hearing about the experiences of others can impact our actions and thoughts. In a growth-mindset classroom, storytelling can reframe failure and mistakes in a positive, energizing way. Start by asking students to process their experiences of successful struggle through quick-writes, journal entries, and longer narrative essays. Then, both teachers and students can verbally share their stories in a small group or with the whole class. Although the examples below focus on failure, you could adapt this strategy to focus on other growth-mindset topics, such as optimism, resilience, flexibility or grit. Potential story prompts might be: "What is something you have quit in your life? What made you quit? Looking back, was it the right decision, or do you wish you would have tried something different?"

- Reproducible #7: Growth-Mindset Personal Narrative (page 156) is a narrative essay assignment that includes a selection of writing prompts around the theme of successful struggle. The student writers will share a difficult experience from which they gained new understanding. This reproducible can be adapted to fit a variety of ages and ability levels.

CHAPTER 12

STRATEGY #9: MAKE TIME FOR REFLECTION

> **CENTRAL GROWTH-MINDSET BELIEF: The practice of honest and purposeful reflection allows students to make sense of and grow from their writing experiences.**

In order to foster growth-mindset thinking, include reflection time after any sustained writing process as an essential aspect of your classroom routine. Reflection provides students the opportunity to truly recognize their continued growth as writers, identify new learning, and identify effective strategies to use in the future.

As a writing instructor, you want your students not only to produce effective writing, but also to understand their writing processes in ways that enable them to replicate success or make appropriate changes. Metacognitive reflection provides an opportunity for them to better understand themselves as writers and to think about their learning processes. They may consider:

- What did I do well?

- What mistakes did I make along the way?

- In what ways was I successful?

- How did my intentions compare with the outcomes?

- What positive changes did I make?

- What new strategies did I gain?

- What new goals do I have for the next writing activity?

In order to truly grow as writers, students must be able to honestly and purposely reflect on the choices surrounding their writing. Reflective practices help develop the dispositions of curious, insightful, flexible writers who can learn from all of their experiences.

Writers must continue to study their writing processes and themselves in order to learn what works best for them. For example, I have watched my students use a variety of strategies during our large research project. Over the years, I have watched some students create organized piles of articles with color-coded Post-it notes, allowing them to focus their attention on one section of the paper at a time. Other students gather all of their books, a laptop, and a 2-liter of Mountain Dew and write nonstop, working intensely for large blocks of time. As experienced writers, we have learned the routines that work best for us, and we do that by reflecting on how we reached success or failure. As they gain new insights, our students can also become active problem solvers, with greater agency to adapt and make changes to better reach the outcomes they seek.

ACTION STEPS

1. USE SHORT GROWTH-MINDSET REFLECTIONS THROUGHOUT THE WRITING PROCESS

Assign students to write short reflections before, during, and after a writing assignment as a quick bell ringer or exit ticket. In the prewriting phase, students might share new goal ideas, brainstorm helpful strategies, and consider potential obstacles they will face in the upcoming writing. If the students anticipate the areas that might pose problems before they begin writing, they may be more successful when they encounter setbacks. In addition, these quick-writes help normalize mistakes, as they let students know that we expect them to make mistakes. It's part of the process!

While drafting, students should continue to analyze their writing processes by identifying their struggles and successes. I like to call these "field notes," a reference to the quick messages a soldier might send back to a superior, providing status updates from the front line of the battle. For teachers, these reflections can serve as formative assessments, guiding their ongoing decisions about instruction. As I read their notes, I try to glean answers to questions like "What can I do to better support their process?" and "What do my students still need?" Such regular meta-cognitive exercises teach students to think about their thinking and writing processes while providing information to guide our decisions about instruction.

Use reflection prompts like the ones below to set goals and activate prior knowledge before a writing cycle, or to assess learning while students are brainstorming, composing, and revising.

EXAMPLE: Growth-Mindset Reflection Prompts

- Right now, what do you believe about your ability as a writer? What mindset do you think these beliefs support?
- What area in the writing process will require the most focus?
- How will putting forth more effort improve your writing process?
- How did you generate your ideas? Was that successful? What other ways could you use?
- How do you plan to write [a specific] section of your paper? What strategies will you use to motivate yourself as you write?

- Where have you been writing outside of class? What distractions are there? What helps you stay focused?

- What other big assignments and plans are you juggling right now? When can you find time to work on your writing this week? Does it work best to schedule a big chunk of time or a little each day?

- What is not working right now? How can I help? How can you help yourself?

- Who will you ask to give you feedback on your writing? Why do you think those people will be helpful?

- When do you typically become frustrated while writing? How can you begin addressing those frustrations earlier?

- What has been your best writing experience? What do you think made that writing so memorable?

2. INCORPORATE SELF-EVALUATION FOR HOLISTIC REFLECTION

Self-evaluations serve as a holistic reflection after the student has completed a writing cycle, portfolio, or semester. Through these reflections, you allow the time and space for students to process their learning. As students reflect on what went well and what didn't, they often gain new insights into who they are as writers. As they acquire new strategies, explore new skills, and develop as writers, they must continue to examine the differences (both positive and negative) these changes have made on their writing outcomes.

When students understand quality criteria for writing and closely examine their own writing, most are able to accurately assess their writing, even proposing a score or grade that they believe they deserve. At the end of a writing cycle or completed unit, allow the writer to process their learning through a self-evaluation. When students reach the point of publication, this reflective practice further emphasizes the importance of the entire learning process, rather than placing all the focus on the final products they have submitted. At the end of a writing cycle, I require my students to submit their brainstorming, early drafts, peer and teacher feedback, and final draft, along with a self-evaluation like the one below, rather than just their final draft. Along the way, they are learning to set new goals, consider strategies for improving their writing, and document their growth. This self-awareness helps students interpret their achievements in ways that will boost their confidence.

I like to start by reading the self-evaluation, and then look back through the student's writing process.

EXAMPLE: Self-Evaluation Assignment

Submit a ½-page, typed response to the following questions when handing in your finished essay:

Describe your process for writing this paper. In what ways did you stick to your usual writing habits? In what ways did you try something new? What worked well? What caused you headaches?

What pleases you about your essay? What part of the paper or the process makes you feel proud?

What elements of your essay would you still like to redo or improve?

What were the benefits of working with your response group? How could we adapt the response group time to make it even more valuable?

Finish these sentences: "I felt _____ after handing in my first paper" because _____." "For my next essay, my goal is to _____."

---

3. ADD REFLECTIONS TO YOUR ASSESSMENT PRACTICES

When assessing student writing (especially in portfolios or end-of-the-year exams), ask students to review and reflect on their entire body of work. Just as athletes watch tapes of prior games or matches, students can reread past essays to gain better insight into their abilities and the trajectory of their growth. When students are assessing a collection of their writing, I also ask them to propose (and defend) their grade for the portfolio.

Each semester, my administration required a final exam in all courses. I always struggled with creating a meaningful exam that supported my beliefs about good writing. Since the students only had two hours to finish the exam, they would not be able to revise or receive feedback. Although I did not want to assign a large writing, my school required the exam to be 10 percent of the semester grade. In order to create an exam that showed rigor but still supported my writing pedagogy, I focused on reflection. The students brought all of their five major writing packets (which include early drafts, peer and teacher feedback, final draft, and self-evaluation for each writing cycle) to the exam period.

During the exam session, they wrote a self-assessment of their work throughout the semester. Rather than adding stress, this exam activity became a way to celebrate their hard work and recognize their impressive growth. While I assigned an exam grade for their self-assessment, I also considered their perspective when deciding their final grade for the course.

- Reproducible #8: Semester Self-Assessment (page 158) is one example of utilizing reflection for a final exam, and it can be easily adapted for other disciplines and grade levels.

4. BUILD A REFLECTIVE WRITING COMMUNITY

Sharing our reflections can be a great way to strengthen the classroom community. When a student shares their reflection with other students, it multiplies the learning taking place. In addition, sharing often validates the experiences of others. When a student shares a frustration or aha moment from their research process, the room often fills with murmurs of "me too" from their classmates. We also offer increased agency as students share their own lessons from their writing process within a community or cohort.

In my college freshman writing course, one of my favorite days was when the students submitted their inquiry-based project, a large assignment that spanned six or seven weeks of intense research and writing. After we consumed boxes of Krispy Kreme donuts, each student shared their takeaways from the writing experience. In such a short time, they learned so much about research, drafting, revision, and publication. It was wonderful to celebrate all of their growth as writers!

On a personal note, many of my most rewarding moments as a writing instructor have come from reading student reflections. When my students share such thoughtful insight about their growth as writers, they validate my work in the most powerful of ways. I received permission from a few of my former students to share their reflections with you.

EXAMPLE: Student Reflection 1

I think as a writer, I am slowly beginning to learn that becoming a good writer takes time and it takes growth. I am also learning my strengths and weaknesses as a writer. Instead of looking down on my weaknesses and getting upset, I've slowly began to use them to shape my writing. Of course, there is always clean up that needs to be done and fixes that need to be made, but I'm able to identify and embrace my weaknesses and instead of trying to fix every mistake immediately, slowly determine how I can continue to grow.

EXAMPLE: Student Reflection 2

I have learned in this class that I still have a lot of growing to do. I learned that I don't always have all of the answers and that I might not always be able to come up with something amazing right away. In fact, I would love to skip this assignment, to not turn anything in, give up and go to sleep. However, I think that is a good sign for developing as a writer. In order to learn new things, I have to be uncomfortable. I have to head out into uncharted waters. At first, I might feel like I am drowning in a new assignment, but I think eventually, with enough persistence and with what I already know as a writer, I will learn to swim and my writing will be far better as a result of my struggle.

EXAMPLE: Student Reflection 3

My writing matters because they are my voice in the world. My writing shows who I am not just as a writer, not just as a student, but who I am as a person. What I write reflects how I feel about a topic…my opinions, my research, my effort, and my skills. Writing gives me the freedom to utilize my style, my vocabulary, my intellect, and my surroundings in order to produce a document that means something to me and can help others.

Both teachers and students should share their reflections to strengthen the classroom community. A teacher friend uses the practice of "Celebrating and Sulking" throughout a writing cycle. Her students focus on the positives during "Celebration Shares," such as writing a great sentence, finding a good source, or finishing a new draft. Sometimes a student announces an aha moment, in which they realized something new about themselves as a writer. One girl found that she writes much better when listening to loud rap music. A classmate discovered a new, quiet coffeehouse (with great coffee!), perfect for working on his writing.

Other days, her students gather for "Sulking Shares," which might include frustration with the introduction, stress over finding time to write, or insecurity about their writing voice. While these sessions often include a lot of laughter, they provide the space and time for students to speak their frustrations and fears. This activity also gives students an opportunity to practice empathy, as the teens listen to their classmates share their struggles and insecurities. If the teacher can remain silent through the sharing, something incredible can often occur. The students begin to offer one another advice, help, and encouragement in their writing. Truly a growth-mindset classroom culture!

CHAPTER 13

STRATEGY #10: USE GROWTH-ORIENTED ASSESSMENT PRACTICES

> **CENTRAL GROWTH-MINDSET BELIEF:** Growth-oriented assessment practices must empower students and measure progress toward mastery rather than define their writing identities.

Every time that I complete a presentation on growth-minded writing instruction, a teacher raises their hand to ask a question about assessment. This is an important concern because growth-mindset beliefs clearly clash with many aspects of traditional assessment practices. While a growth-oriented pedagogy encourages risk, recognizes effort, and values process over product, the A to F system is often decided by one-shot tests and papers. Moreover, letter grades do not provide a clear picture of student learning, as they are frequently altered by completion grades and extra credit points. Even a parent who strongly advocates for traditional grades would likely struggle to explain what a B communicates about their child's writing ability.

Historically, the assessment of student writing occurs at the end of the unit, after the learning has occurred, with no chance of revision. Given that teachers need time to grade the papers, the teacher's feedback for the writer is often delayed for at least a few days and is seldom used for revision of the piece. In addition, the summative assessment grades only provide a snapshot of each learner at one moment in time, rather than a comprehensive look at their writing development. Most likely, the student has written about a topic that did not interest them, for an inauthentic purpose, and to an audience of only one: the teacher. Clearly, the values communicated through this type of assessment are not aligned with a growth-mindset or writing pedagogy and reflect larger problems in traditional grading practices.

In the book and feature-length documentary *Most Likely to Succeed*, education experts Tony Wagner and Ted Dintersmith provide a scathing critique of education today, which includes the position that "today, assessment in our schools has become the bitter enemy of learning."[63]

CONSIDER!

How can writing instructors alter the grading process to communicate a growth-mindset message? How can our writing assessments recognize growth, reward effort, and value the students' progress as much as the final products?

While I recognize the importance of assessing student learning, traditional grading practices can be problematic for a growth-mindset classroom. First, students with fixed-minded beliefs view assessments as a significant threat that will likely result in failure and embarrassment. Just like you would dread a tennis match if you were trying to hide a weak serve, "bad writers" are terrified of submitting their final papers, as the final assessment may reveal their lack of ability. Rather than receiving a low grade—which would only confirm their inadequacy—fixed-minded writers put forth low effort, blame others, or just don't submit their writing at all. According to Dweck, when teachers are judging them, students will sabotage the teacher's effort to assess by not trying.[64]

While many fixed-minded students exert as little effort as possible, others become obsessed with looking smart. For these students, a letter grade becomes a confirmation of where they rank as writers. Rather than offering a measure of progress, grades have the power to determine one's identity, separating the winners from the losers. Once grades become the primary motivator, students will mainly focus on points and percentages, feel anxiety about writing assignments, and fall apart when they receive low grades. The pressure to perform kills any opportunity for curiosity and creativity.

Given the relationship between assessment and mindsets, I avoid using letter grades to evaluate student writing whenever possible. Letter grades do not foster growth-mindset thinking, nor do they help our students become better writers. They are more likely to scare students away from writing, damage their confidence, and cause increased anxiety. It's not surprising that students are uncomfortable taking risks and accepting failure in an educational environment where their shortcomings will be recorded as low letter grades.

GROWTH-MINDSET WRITING ASSESSMENT WITHIN A TRADITIONAL SYSTEM

While alternative approaches are gaining momentum, massive educational reform comes slowly. The reality is that most of us work in a school district that requires us to submit letter grades, which are used for transcripts, class ranking, intervention resources, and school accreditation. However, college acceptance and tuition costs create the greatest pressure for high grades, leading students to prize an A more than learning and other types of engagement, including creativity and imagination. In higher education today, a student's GPA is the single most influential factor in determining acceptance into competitive college programs.[65] Grades and standardized test scores also influence scholarships, a factor that cannot be overlooked since the average university costs between $20,000 and $40,000 per year.

As long as university admission programs continue to value grades, we cannot simply discount their role in student learning. However, we can still be intentional about how, what, and why we grade in the writing classroom. While you may work in a system that requires traditional grading, you can still incorporate growth-mindset beliefs into your assessment practices, creating conditions that allow for struggle, highlight growth, and value process over product.

If you must assign grades, here are a few ways to incorporate growth-mindset beliefs into a traditional grading system, creating the best conditions for assessing writers:

• Grade writing less, assess writing more. Not every piece of writing needs a grade. Student writing should be regularly assessed for learning, but assessment is not synonymous with grading. Developing writers need a lot of time to practice and experiment with the moves that will improve writing; they need frequent and purposeful low-stakes writing activities. This regular writing time might include brainstorming, working on drafts, or writing activities that follow mini-lessons. This time is critical to student growth, as it allows our students to take risks, try new approaches, and struggle without fear of consequences. These day-to-day writings are ungraded, but that doesn't mean they should be ignored. Offer timely and regular feedback on drafts so students can use your critiques as they revise. These writings can also be used as formative assessments to help gauge your students' understanding, especially when you are introducing new skills. By assessing short writing samples, you determine the content and the pace of future instruction, recognize the need for differentiation, and identify which learners need additional support.

- Reserve letter grades for summative assessments when evaluating mastery of the content at the end of a unit or writing phase, such as tests, final drafts, exams, and projects. Most daily work occurs while students are still learning new skills or material. If you want students to embrace challenges or take risks in their learning, they should not be penalized for making mistakes. By separating academic assessments from participation and low-stakes completion points, you can also make sure that the letter grade provides a clearer picture of a student's mastery of the writing skills. When you are using a letter grade on a summative assessment, you can also incorporate mastery-level language to clarify to students what a grade means for their learning.

Example: Master-Level Language		
NUMBER SCORE	TRADITIONAL GRADE	MASTERY LANGUAGE
4	A+	Exceeding expectations with skills and abilities
3	A to B-	Meeting expectations with skills and abilities
2	C+ to D	Developing skills and abilities
1	D- or below	Beginning with skills and abilities

- Evaluate the process, rather than the product. One problem with most summative assessments is that they tell us how a student performed during short time span on one particular day, rather than providing a holistic view of the student's progress and growth. In a growth-oriented classroom, summative assessments would focus on the growth and effort throughout the overall process, rather than one final product. Even the Common Core State Standards recognize the importance of writing, which asks students to "write routinely over extended time frames (time for research, reflection, and revision)."[66]

Rather than just collecting a final draft, I ask my students to turn in a folder for each writing unit, which includes the following materials: brainstorming activities, early drafts, peer and teacher feedback, revised draft, and a self-reflection. (I hate the phrase "final draft," because we can always continue revising a work.) The letter grade is based on their writing development throughout the unit, rather than the "correctness" of the final draft.

- When I present at staff workshops or conferences, teachers often share the ways that they have altered their grading approach to include more growth-mindset criteria. They want to make sure that all students work hard to achieve an A, and they also want to make sure students who improve are rewarded for their effort. One teacher explained how she carefully reviews a student's revision work when assigning an essay grade, basing a quarter of the paper grade on the growth shown throughout the writing process. Another teacher adds a "mindset score" into each student's overall grade, which is based on mindset behaviors or dispositions, such as showing grit in the face of difficulty, seeking out feedback from others, and setting challenging writing goals throughout the semester. Still other teachers have revised their rubrics to include a "mindset" or "growth" category to communicate the importance of embracing challenge, recovering from setbacks, and showing effort.

There are many creative approaches to assessing student work that support research-based beliefs about writing and encourage growth-mindset thinking. When grades can be seen as feedback for learning, rather than a system to rate one performance against others, your students will be able to recognize writing as a process, one in which all writers have more to learn.

ACTION STEPS

1. EXPLORE ALTERNATIVE ASSESSMENTS

Instead of letter grades, use alternative forms of evaluation to monitor and report learning, including student-led conferences, learning contracts, and teacher narratives. Many progressive colleges and K–12 districts have abandoned traditional tests and letter grades for new models of authentic and personalized assessment, with the hope that the absence of traditional letter grades will increase student motivation while maintaining rigor and excellence.

Alternative assessments like the following monitor student learning while still motivating students to push beyond their comfort zone.

Student-Led Conferences: Rather than excluding students from the conversation, you can put them in charge. In a student-led conference, students meet with you and their parents to review their writing goals, the obstacles they have encountered, and the progress they have made. By including students in the conference, we focus the conversation on their experiences, feelings, thoughts, and opinions, rather than just reviewing the grade book with the parents. Student-led conferences provide students with more agency, while giving parents additional insight into the growth of their child.

Digital Reading or Writing Portfolios: Students create a digital portfolio of their best work—essays, poetry, short stories, projects, and even artwork—to demonstrate mastery of the most important skills. Portfolios could be evaluated by qualified teachers as well as experts from the community. The evaluations would offer students feedback, identify areas for improvement, and suggest direction for the future. Ideally, portfolios could be shared on college admission applications and job interviews.

Teacher Narratives: Narrative assessments are written by the teacher to discuss a student's work, learning, and growth throughout a semester. The narratives are sent home to the student's family and made available to other teachers, counselors, and administrators. All of the student narratives are kept in a large portfolio of their work.

Narratives often focus on the student's writing goals, learning standards, and writing portfolios. Reflect on student progress in each of these areas and highlight their personal qualities, work habits, and potential goals for the next semester. Adjust the length and frequency of the narratives depending on the number of students in your class. You might also consider using different formats, such as verbal narratives captured on a voice recorder, to save time and energy. Since many teachers post grades online, a verbal narrative assessment could also be communicated during parent-teacher conferences.

Publications and Exhibitions: Rather than using letter grades to motivate student learning, create authentic writing assignments, ones in which the students will be publishing their final drafts or creating public presentations for community members. You can use project- and community-based learning units, which require students to write for real audiences and purposes. You can also hold exhibitions at the end of each learning term, in which students show their best work to a panel of their teachers, parents, peers, and community mentors. When the audience for their writing moves beyond the classroom walls, students are motivated to give their best and be held accountable for their learning.

2. ASSESS FOR MASTERY USING STANDARDS-BASED GRADING

The way you evaluate your students' work can also help them develop a growth mindset. When students don't master a particular skill, consider giving them a grade of "Not Yet" or "Developing" Instead of a failing grade. This way, learning is not confined to a particular time window.

Although the majority of schools are still using letter grades, forty-eight states have adopted policies to promote a shift toward standards- or competency-based grading.[67] As with the example above, these approaches do not use scores, percentages, or letter grades, but instead assess student growth by indicating where their work falls on a spectrum (e.g., little to no mastery, partial mastery, proficient, advanced). If a student does not meet mastery, the teacher will use additional interventions or reteach the material, supporting the student until they master the targeted skills.

With standards-based grading, assessments focus on learning and clearly communicate progress to the students and parents. While standards-based grading can be converted into letter grades (e.g., partial mastery = C+), this assessment approach is significantly different from traditional grading in that it allows for ongoing revision and the opportunity to improve until mastery is met. Standards-based grading better supports growth-mindset beliefs, recognizing that all students do not learn at the same pace, but with effort and support, they can all have the potential to reach mastery.

When using a standards-based approach, make sure to give students feedback during the learning process and allow them more than just one opportunity to demonstrate their skills. That approach works quite well in a writing classroom, as you are able to provide ongoing support through multiple drafts and individual conferences. However, standards-based grading can also be used to assess literature skills through writing.

- Reproducible #9: Standards-Based Literature Assessment (page 160) is a unit test that asks students to write short responses to demonstrate their mastery of five ELA Literature Standards. The questions require students to apply their literacy skills, rather than recount specific symbols, themes, or characters from one particular novel.

Although my students were familiar with a standards-based approach, I included a brief summary of the scoring procedure at the top of the test. After collecting the tests, I assigned a score of 1 to 4 for each question, representing the student's level of mastery for each skill. Often, students show mastery in three or four skills, but not all five. During the following week, the students can be given additional support or resources, individually or in small groups, until they are able to demonstrate mastery in all five standards.

3. INCORPORATE GROWTH-MINDSET VALUES INTO A LETTER-GRADE SYSTEM

In summative assessments, teachers take a more holistic look at student progress by evaluating growth throughout an entire writing cycle or series of writings, rather than just one final product. Consider ways to reward growth-mindset behaviors, like adapting rubrics to include a score for growth, reflection, or other growth-mindset values.

- Reproducible #10: Personal Narrative Rubric (page 164) uses mastery language to assess Reproducible #7: Growth-Mindset Personal Narrative (page 156) and includes a revision section to evaluate the student's use of new writing approaches and feedback through their writing process. Since my feedback is focused on next steps that will challenge the writer to grow, I reward points for embracing that challenge, regardless of whether it works out perfectly. I would rather my students try new approaches in their writing and fail miserably than coast along on safe, perfect papers.

- Reproducible #11: Single-Point Rubric (page 166) offers another way to incorporate growth-mindset thinking into writing assessment. When reviewing a student's draft, you could use this rubric to provide clear feedback. If a student has reached mastery for a requirement, place a check mark in the "You Got It!" column and make note of how the criteria was met. In areas that require additional effort, check "Not Yet!" and follow up through a conference with the student to make sure additional resources and support are in place. Brock and Hundley point out that teachers use a top-down approach to rubrics, prescribing the "right way to do a task, activity, or assignment" in the meets expectation and exceeds expectations categories.[68] Single-point rubrics are more authentic for writing tasks as they invite students to demonstrate mastery in a variety of ways.

- Reproducible #12: Writing Process Performance Rubric (page 167) moves the focus from assessing skills and standards to noncognitive competencies. This rubric highlights growth-mindset behaviors and dispositions that we want to nurture in our students until they are able to move through the writing process independently. This rubric would be a great source of formative feedback for students to review before they create new writing goals!

FINAL WORDS

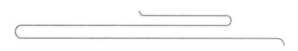

"Everyone has the capacity to write, writing can be taught, and teachers can help students become better writers."

—NCTE Beliefs about the Teaching of Writing[69]

Over my last fifteen years as a writing teacher, I have met many, many students who saw themselves as bad writers—not because they were unmotivated or did not care, but because they believed they lacked the ability to write well. This continued to bother me because I viewed these students much differently. To me, they were developing writers with great potential. If they were willing to put in the time and effort to use new strategies, listen to feedback from others, and remain persistent through failure, they would be successful writers. The main difference between their perspective and mine? Mindset.

In a publication in *Nature*, Dweck and colleagues clarify that just teaching students about mindsets is not enough. Student beliefs are also impacted by other factors in the school environment, such as teacher training.[70] In other words: context is critical. Pinning a poster about growth mindset on the wall of a classroom does not help if the teacher creates an environment where kids are terrified of making a mistake. According to Dweck, "the environment has to support the belief change and the behaviors that come with it."[71]

Students' writing identities are influenced by the messages from their writing teacher and classroom environment. If you want to foster growth-minded thinking, begin by reflecting on the daily choices that you make and the teaching practices that shape your student writers. Then, build a community where all your students can, with effort and support, become successful writers. In order to convince your students of their potential, embed positive-mindset messages within all aspects of your classroom culture. While concepts like modeling, process feedback, or reflection are not new to writing pedagogy, you can reimagine these best practices through a growth-mindset lens. Through intentional goal setting, responsive feedback, thoughtful assessment, and other growth-oriented instructional strategies, you repeatedly encourage positive identities and mindset beliefs that help beginning writers grow rather than hold them back.

When you cultivate a growth-oriented classroom culture, you can alter the way your students see their writing, and help them see themselves as writers. As students come to understand their abilities through the lens of effort and growth, they embrace—rather than resist—the complex process of writing. I don't want my students to aim for perfect writing or to master the writing process, I just want them to continue to grow. As Kristine Mraz and Christine Hertz succinctly state: "We are never done; we are only ever doing."[72]

Use a mindset approach to maximize not only your students' growth as writers, but also their dispositions as resilient, curious, confident, and reflective people. By embracing growth-minded beliefs, your students can view themselves as capable writers, take ownership of their abilities, and find the confidence to keep writing for the rest of their lives.

APPENDIX

REPRODUCIBLE #1: Brainstorming My Writing Goal
(Student Handout)

Name: _____

Date: _____ Class: _____

Get Ready to Grow!

What Do I Want to Accomplish with My Writing?	What Are My Strengths & Areas of Confidence?
What Are My Speed Bumps & Concrete Walls?	**What Resources Do I Have to Help Me Grow?**

If "10" is where you want to be as a writer, where would you place yourself now? Why? What do you think will help you get to a "10"?

1   2   3   4   5   6   7   8   9   1 0

Beginning to Experienced Writer

REPRODUCIBLE #2: My Writing SMART Goal
(Student Handout)

Name: _____

Date: _____ Class: _____

SMART Goal Template

Current Reality (What do I desire to change?)

SMART Goal (What might be some ways to change that reality?)

Anticipated Outcome (How will I know that I have been successful in changing those realities?)

HOW DOES MY GOAL FULFILL SMART GOAL CRITERIA?

Specific?

Measurable?

Actionable?

Realistic?

Timely?

PLANNING & PROGRESS NOTES

Conference Date:

Discussion Topics

What Resources or Strategies Do I Need?

What Are My Next Steps?

REFLECTION ON GOAL PROCESS

Consider the following questions:

How was your goal work successful?

What would you do differently next time around?

What unexpected barriers or problems did you run into?

What was a new resource or strategy you found?

How have you grown as a writer?

REPRODUCIBLE #3: Individual Writing Profile
(Teacher Documentation)

Individual Writing Profile

RESULTS OF MINDSET SURVEY & MINDSET CHARACTERISTICS OBSERVED		
Early Semester	Middle of Semester	End of Semester

WRITING SAMPLE ANALYSIS
Sample
Strengths
Areas for Growth

WRITING SAMPLE ANALYSIS
Sample
Strengths
Areas for Growth

STUDENT WRITING GOALS		
Early Semester	Middle of Semester	End of Semester

INDIVIDUAL WRITING CONFERENCES			
Date	Student Concerns	Teacher Feedback	Strategies & Resources

REPRODUCIBLE #4: Response Groups Assignment
(Student Handout)

Response Groups Assignment

Next to writing, taking part in a response group is the most important activity we do in a writing workshop classroom!

PART I: Meet in Response Groups during class, following this routine:

1) Each writer will bring enough copies of their essay for members of the response group. Each writer will also prepare two questions or areas of concern for their response group to address.

2) Once response group time begins, each writer will read their piece to the group. The other group members will annotate the piece for areas they can complement and suggestions.

3) After the writer has read their piece, they will pose their questions to the group. The group will then spend time giving suggestions and discussing the work, *without input from the author*. Remember to use the stance of an admirer or a friendly reader.

• Not sure what to say? Try using these comment stems…

• My favorite part/sentence/image in the writing is

_____

_____

because _____

• When I read this part _____

it makes me wonder _____

• I am confused by _____

___

• I am wondering what would happen if the author changed/switched

_____

- As a reader, I would love to hear more about _____

  _____

- I think _____could be

  cut down or maybe left out because _____

4) Then, the next writer will read, with the same cycle.

5) Each group member will then write or type out a response *on a separate piece of paper for each person's paper*. They will be giving one full sheet to each person.

PART II: Write Response Letter to Each Group Member

This response should be conversational, written in sentences that make sense. Your papers should have headings and be addressed clearly on the top line in the center.

To: _____ (group member's name): Include the date of the response group and the editor's name (you). Then take time to reread your group member's draft once again, and write out the following in your letter:

1) Begin with "reading back" your impressions of the work—summarize what you understand as the general ideas in the essay as a whole.

  » Be sure to mention which *specific* portions of the work give you the strongest impression of what's "happening" in the writing.

  » Then write what you consider to be the main purpose(s) of the writing. What is the author trying to achieve?

2) Offer praise for the paper's strengths, and comment on things you learned from reading the paper. Write out what is effective in the piece, which will be combined with your annotations on the copy of the draft.

3) Offer constructive suggestions about things that the author didn't ask you to consider but that you feel might be helpful. Ask questions; point out confusions. Remember to use "I" statements: "I feel like I need more details in the first stanza to really understand what's happening," as opposed to "you should add more information to the first stanza." Again—combine this with annotating the text.

4) Respond to things the author asked you to consider.

5) Sign your annotated copy of each piece and staple it to your comments for that person. If there are a total of four of you in a response group, you'll hand in three separate stapled bundles.

Response Group Assessment

_____ /15	_____ /10
1-page response letter to each author, addressing overall purpose, successful areas, & points for improvement	Response letter feedback points to specific sections, lines, & word choice

_____ /15	_____ /10
Paper copy includes annotations, comments edited for stylistic & mechanical mistakes	Active participation in Response Group conversation during class time

TOTAL SCORE	_____ /50

REPRODUCIBLE #5: Talk Back to Fixed-Mindset Thoughts (Student Handout)

Name: _____

Date: _____ Class: _____

FIXED-MINDSET THOUGHT	TALK BACK!
I can't think of anything to write. I might as well give up!	You can't think of anything to write yet! How about asking your teacher for some brainstorming strategies?
I can never get started writing.	You know the steps to start! Let's just try!
My papers are always horrible.	You may have made mistakes before, but you can learn and change!
Why would they want feedback from me? I'll just make their paper worse.	
She is a better writer than I am.	
My ideas are dumb. I'll sound stupid if I share them with anyone else.	
This writing assignment is too hard.	

FIXED-MINDSET THOUGHT	TALK BACK!
I can never come up with a good introduction or conclusion.	
Who cares about citation anyway?	
My rough draft is good enough.	
There's no way I am going to be able to finish this entire writing assignment anyway.	
I don't know what to fix.	
No one cares about what I have to say.	
My writing will never be any good.	

REPRODUCIBLE #6: Verse Novel Project
(Student Handout)

Verse Novel Project

Directions: Choose one of the following options for your verse novel final project. Projects will be assessed on overall effort, creativity, and your understanding of your verse novel. You must complete all elements of the project as they are listed below. There are many options available, but any changes to these options must be preapproved. All of the projects require a similar amount of time and effort (so don't look too hard for the "easy" one!) Take time to review each option and choose your project based on your level of interest and/or hobbies.

Build the Playlist: Make a fifteen-song playlist to be published with your verse novel. Each song must represent a different verse in the novel. The project must include a typed paper in which you explain why you are including each of the songs on the playlist. For each song or musical piece, write a paragraph in which you explain connection between the lyrics and/or music to themes, symbols, and/or characters in the verse, using textual evidence (quotes from the verse) to show the similarities. The songs should go in the order of the verses from the novel. Requirements: (1) fifteen songs minimum (artist/song title) for playlist; (2) a one-paragraph explanation for each song: use the lyrics of the song to explain how it relates to the themes, symbols, and/or characters from the verse novel.

Write Fan Fiction: Write a piece of short fiction in which you take a character from your verse novel and transport them. You can bring the character to a new time period (such as ten years after the story ends), new genre (vampire romance perhaps?), or new location. Try, as best you can, to replicate and emulate the character's unique voice. You do not have to write it in the style of the play but can instead write it like a popular fiction novel or short story. Be creative! Try to use what you know of the character to guide your story line, and incorporate details from the real verse novel to guide your new story. Refer back to the verse novel, using flashbacks, characters, or similar conflicts. Quote when possible and maintain the major themes of the play. Requirements: (1) five-to-seven-page story with the same central characters from your verse novel, but with a unique twist!

Compose Music or Poetry: Write five original songs or poems that illustrate meaningful scenes from the verse novel. For each song/poem, be sure to include a two-paragraph explanation (minimum) that connects your lyrics to themes, symbols, and/or characters in the verse novel, using textual evidence (quotes from the verse) to show the similarities. A candy bar will be given to the songwriter who can compose the music to accompany the lyrics. Please prepare to share one poem or song with the class (either live or from a recorded performance of the song/poem). Requirements: (1) five original songs or poems; (2) two paragraphs about each song or poem, explaining how the lyrics of the song/poem compare to the themes, symbols, and/or characters from the verse novel.

Cast the Film: Congratulations! You have just been hired to produce a play or cast the movie production of your verse novel. Identify the main characters from your verse novel and then select the popular celebrities to fit each of the main roles. Then, announce your production with an eye-catching poster, including dates and times of performances, location of performances, and names and pictures of your stars. Be creative! Write a one-paragraph report per character, explaining why you chose that character for his/her role. What characteristics does this actor have that exemplifies the corresponding character in your verse novel? How does that actor possess physical characteristics, personality traits, or prior roles that correlate to the character from your novel? Be sure to use evidence from the text in your explanations! Requirements: (1) six character castings; (2) a one-paragraph explanation per character, using the verse novel to explain the reason why the actor correlates with the look, personality, or mood of the character in the verse novel; (3) a movie poster advertising the production that includes images and text. This may be done on posterboard and drawn by hand or created online through Glogster.

Create Pinterest Board: Create a Pinterest Board from the perspective of the main character in your verse novel. You must include fifteen different pins on your board and write a one-paragraph caption under each pin, explaining how the pin relates to the character's interests, values, experiences, or dreams. Write each pin in the character's voice and include specific evidence from the text. Be creative! What tattoo would they be considering? Which quote would be their inspiration? Which clothing would they be checking out? Requirements: (1) fifteen pins on a character Pinterest board; (2) a one-paragraph explanation for each pin in the caption using first-person perspective to explain the connection between the pin and the central character in the verse novel.

Do you have another idea? Write a one-page proposal explaining how you will use a different creative genre to analyze the central themes and characters in your verse novel. Your proposal must be approved before you begin your project!

REPRODUCIBLE #7: Growth-Mindset Personal Narrative (Student Handout)

Personal Narrative Assignment

Purpose: This assignment asks you to reflect on a situation in which you experienced productive failure, struggled but learned a valuable lesson, or grew as a person in a positive way.

Directions: Carefully read the prompts below. Then, select one of the prompts to write a personal narrative that responds to it completely.

Narrative Prompts for Writing (Select One Topic for Writing):

Describe a time you struggled or received a low grade in a class. Explain how you reacted at that time. How do you feel looking back at it now? What did you learn from this experience, and how will it help you in the future?

Think about a time when you faced a social or personal challenge. How did you respond? In what ways did the experience change you? How can you use it as an opportunity for growth?

Talk about a time when you quit something. What made you quit? Looking back, do you wish you would have tried something different? If so, explain. If not, explain what you learned from quitting this activity/task.

Write a brief story about a time you failed at something you worked really hard on. How did it make you feel? How does it impact how you approach situations today? What did you learn from this experience?

Describe something that took you a long time to learn or understand. How often did you want to give up? What do you think motivated you to keep trying? What resources did you use? Tell me about the moment when you finally figured it out.

Write about a time when you gave less than your best effort. What was your reasoning for doing so? Was the outcome what you expected it to be? What did you learn from that experience?

Describe how a teacher, coach, or mentor taught you an important lesson in your life. What were you struggling with before they stepped in? How did that lesson change who you are or the choices that you make?

REPRODUCIBLE #8: Semester Self-Assessment
(Student Handout)

"Myself as Writer"

Directions: For your final writing for this course, use the allotted time to compose an essay assessing yourself as a writer. In your essay, use paragraphs, complete sentences, and organized thoughts. You should not view your essay answers as a series of free-writes or journaling. You do not need to answer every question in the prompts below, but use the questions as a guide for content of your response.

Objectives:

Evaluate the strategies, resources, and habits that have guided your writing process.

Assess your strengths, identify potential areas for future writing goals, and celebrate your growth during this course.

Articulate how your writing ability informs your identity; understand critical thinking, reading, and writing as means to learn, work, and advocate throughout your life.

Assignment:

In this essay, you have the opportunity to evaluate and analyze yourself and your writing process. First, start by discussing how you have seen your strengths and weaknesses as a writer in the past, including frustrations and successes, your positive and negative experiences with writing and writing teachers, your previous approaches to drafting and revision, and your own relationship with academic, creative, and personal writing.

Then, shift your perspective to evaluating some of those same elements now, while also considering how you have evolved and grown: How has your perception of yourself as writer shifted from Day 1 of class to today? What do you believe are your strengths? In what areas would you still like to grow? What new strategies have you found work best for your writing process? What habits are you trying to let go of? What do you wish you would have done differently in this course?

Finally, take time to look forward. What are your writing goals for next year and life after school? How will you continue to grow as a writer? What are the takeaways that you will remember from this class? What skills, strategies, and lessons from our class might be valuable to your future classes, in your workplace, and during your social communication? And finally...why do you believe your writing matters?

REPRODUCIBLE #9: Standards-Based Literature
Assessment (Student Handout)

Literature Assessment

Directions: Please answer the following questions in each section. Use complete sentences and support all of your answers with details from the text. When you are quoting directly from the text, set them apart with quotation marks and include the page number.

For each response, you will receive a score 1 to 4, which translates as:

SCORE	SKILL LEVEL
4	Exceeds Expectation for Target Skill
3	Meets Expectation for Target Skill
2	Partial Mastery of Target Skill
1	Little to No Mastery

On the sections that you receive a 3 or 4, you have reached mastery for that skill and will receive full points on the assessment.

On the sections that you receive a 1 or 2, we will keep working together until you reach mastery. In my feedback, I will give you instructions on when we will meet next. Please let me know if you have any additional questions.

Essay Questions

CCSS.ELA-LITERACY.RL.11-12.1   Score: _____

1) Answer two of the following opinion questions and use textual evidence to support your answers.

» Imagine your friend is considering reading this book and asks your opinion. What do you tell them? Use specific details so you will be convincing!

» What mental pictures has the author created for you? How have they been fully developed?

» For which characters do you feel sympathy and/or empathy? What details make you feel that way?

» Which characters did you connect with the most? What makes these characters likable and relatable?

» At the end of the book, have any of the characters truly changed? Explain your answer.

» Talk specifically about the ending of the book. What do you wish the author would have done differently? Why?

» Which image, scene, or quote in the novel stood out to you the most? Explain why.

CCSS.ELA-LITERACY.RL.11-12. 1   Score: _____

2) Select two themes or central ideas from the options and analyze their development over the course of the text, including how they interact and build on one another to produce a complete narrative.

[Teacher can provide 4-6 themes if using an anchor text(s)]

CCSS.ELA-LITERACY.RL.11-12.3   Score: _____

3) Choose one dynamic character in the novel. Discuss both *how* and *why* the character changes throughout the course of the novel. How is the character's growth important to the overall novel?

[Teacher can provide 4-6 characters if using an anchor text(s)]

CCSS.ELA-LITERACY.RL.11-12.4   Score: _____

4) Analyze how one literary device is used through the novel. Select one literary device and identify where the author uses the device in the novel. Why did the author choose to use this device rather than others? Why is the device used in a particular scene or section? How does the device impact the reader's experience with the novel?

[Teacher can provide 3-5 literary devices if using an anchor text(s)]

5) Determine the point of view of the main narrator or central focalizer. What is he or she trying to communicate to the reader? How does his or her style (word choice, sentence arrangement, tone) and perspective (what we know of characters, events, internal dialogue) contribute to the power, persuasiveness, or beauty of the text?

REPRODUCIBLE #10: Personal Narrative Rubric
(Student Assessment)

CRITERIA	ADVANCED (5)	SHOWS MASTERY (4)
Creativity/ Engagement	Memorable, engaging story with vibrant sensory details & descriptions	Clear narrative story that includes many details & descriptions
Clarity, Flow, & Organization	Well organized, logical, flows smoothly, and clearly articulated; connects ideas smoothly	Organized, logical, flows somewhat smoothly, and clearly articulated; transitions often connect ideas smoothly
Style/Voice	Sophisticated variety of sentences; rich word choice, precise & concise	Variety of sentences; effective word choice, mostly precise & concise
Grammar/ Mechanics	Demonstrates high level of proficiency concerning grammar & mechanics, with no errors	Demonstrates proficiency concerning grammar & mechanics, with very few errors
Insight	Shows elevated level of insight in terms of personal experience and impact	Shows high level of insight in terms of personal experience and impact, while more development is needed
Growth-Mindset Factors	Impressive revision, effort, and growth!	Significant revision, used feedback and some new strategies. Good effort!

SKILL DEVELOPING (3)	SKILL BEGINNING (2)	NEEDS INTERVENTION (1)
Storyline ranges from interesting to common throughout this piece	Ideas are common or cliché; lacks details & descriptions	Idea is a copy of another work or is not personal
Mainly organized and logical, abrupt flow, and somewhat articulate; transitions sometimes used to connect ideas	Lacks organization, logic, flow, and clarity; transitions seldom used to connect ideas	Not organized or clear; doesn't use transitions to connect ideas
Some variety of sentences; appropriate word choice, somewhat precise & concise	Mostly simple sentences; simple word choice, struggles with precision	Only simple sentences; inappropriate word choice, lack of precision
Demonstrates sufficient level of proficiency concerning grammar & mechanics	Demonstrates basic level of proficiency concerning grammar & mechanics	Grammar and mechanics at a deficient level
Shows adequate level of insight in terms of personal experience and impact	Shows minimal level of insight	Shows lack of insight; inability to perceive/ interpret
Some revision from teacher and feedback.; some growth and effort evident in the process	Minimal revision and little growth shown; needs to increase effort	No revision after feedback; the writer gave up without effort

REPRODUCIBLE #11: Single-Point Rubric
(Student Assessment)

Name: _____

Date: _____ Class: _____

NOT YET	REQUIREMENTS	YOU GOT IT!
	Claim This essay has a thesis statement that directly states the main claim of the essay.	
	Evidence The main claim is supported by convincing evidence in the following paragraphs.	
	Appeals The writer has used at least one appeal (ethos, pathos, logos) to support the argument.	
	Grammar The reader is not distracted or confused by grammatical errors.	
	Citation All sources are cited within paper and in Works Cited.	

REPRODUCIBLE #12: Writing Process Performance Rubric (Student Assessment)

	INDEPENDENT PERFORMANCE	PERFORMANCE WITH SUPPORT	NOT YET PERFORMED
Sets Goals	Student can work toward a new writing goal independently.	Student works toward a new writing goal with guided support.	Student is not working toward a new writing goal yet.
Accepts Challenge	Student accepts a new challenge with enthusiasm.	Student accepts a new challenge with reluctance.	Student is not willing to accept a new challenge yet.
Uses Positive Self-Talk	Student uses positive language to speak about their writing abilities.	Student mostly uses positive language to speak about their writing abilities.	Student uses negative language to speak about their writing abilities.
Takes Risks	Student is willing to try new writing styles and strategies.	Student is willing to try new writing styles and strategies with support.	Student is not yet willing to try new writing styles and strategies.
Seeks Out Feedback	Student asks others for feedback on their writing.	Student asks others for feedback on their writing when prompted by the teacher.	Student is not yet willing to share their writing with others.
Tries New Strategies	Student is able to use a variety of strategies when struggling.	Student is able to use strategies, when the strategies are suggested by the teacher.	Student is not yet able to use strategies when struggling.

	INDEPENDENT PERFORMANCE	PERFORMANCE WITH SUPPORT	NOT YET PERFORMED
Asks for Help	Student asks for help when needed.	Student asks for help when prompted by the teacher.	Student is not yet able to ask for help.
Reflects on Learning	Student is able to reflect on writing process independently.	Student is able to reflect on writing process when the prompts or questions are provided.	Student is not yet able to reflect on writing process.

COMMON CORE STANDARDS ALIGNMENT CHART

This growth-mindset resource aligns with the values embedded throughout all CCSS disciplines, such as an emphasis on using multiple processes and procedures; presenting opportunities to approach a text, situation, or problem from multiple angles; making new connections; and challenging the brain.

COLLEGE AND CAREER READINESS ELA ANCHOR STANDARDS FOR WRITING	
CCSS.ELA-LITERACY.W. 2	Write informative/explanatory texts to examine and convey complex ideas, concepts, and information clearly and accurately through the effective selection, organization, and analysis of content.
CCSS.ELA-LITERACY.W.3	Write narratives to develop real or imagined experiences or events using effective technique, well-chosen details, and well-structured event sequences.
CCSS.ELA-LITERACY.W.4	Produce clear and coherent writing to which the development, organization, and style are appropriate to task, purpose, and audience.
CCSS.ELA-LITERACY.W.10	Write routinely over extended time frames (time for research, reflection, and revision) and shorter time frames (a single sitting or a day or two) for a range of tasks, purposes, and audiences.
COLLEGE AND CAREER READINESS ELA ANCHOR STANDARDS FOR LANGUAGE	
CCSS.ELA-LITERACY.L.1	Demonstrate command of the conventions of standard English grammar and usage when writing or speaking.
CCSS.ELA-LITERACY. L.2	Demonstrate command of the conventions of standard English capitalization, punctuation, and spelling when writing.

NOTES

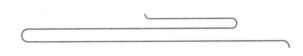

1.   Lisa S. Blackwell, Kali H. Trzesniewski, and Carol S. Dweck, "Implicit Theories of Intelligence Predict Achievement across an Adolescent Transition: A Longitudinal Study and an Intervention," *Child Development* 78, no. 1 (January 2007): 258–59; Carol S. Dweck and Daniel C. Molden, "Self-Theories: Their Impact on Competence Motivation and Acquisition," in *Handbook of Competence and Motivation*, ed. Andrew J. Elliot and Carol S. Dweck (New York: Guilford Press, 2005), 123. David S. Yeager and Carol S. Dweck, "Mindsets that Promote Resilience: When Students Believe that Personal Characteristics Can Be Developed," *Educational Psychologist* 47, no. 4 (October 2012): 313.

2.   Daniel C. Molden and Carol S. Dweck, "Finding 'Meaning' in Psychology: A Lay Theories Approach to Self-Regulation, Social Perception, and Social Development," *American Psychologist* 61, no. 3 (April 2006): 192; Heidi Grant and Carol S. Dweck, "Clarifying Achievement Goals and their Impact," *Journal of Personality and Social Psychology* 85, no. 3 (September 2003): 541–53.

3.   Carol S. Dweck, *Mindset: The New Psychology of Success* (New York: Ballantine Books, 2006), 12.

4.   Catherine Good, Aneeta Rattan, and Carol S. Dweck. "Why Do Women Opt Out? Sense of Belonging and Women's Representation in Mathematics," *Journal of Personality and Social Psychology* 102, no. 4 (April 2012): 714; Grant and Dweck, "Clarifying Achievement Goals," 550–52; Blackwell, Trzesniewski, and Dweck, "Implicit Theories," 258; Catherine Good, Joshua Aronson, and Michael Inzlicht, "Improving Adolescents' Standardized Test Performance: An Intervention to Reduce the Effects of Stereotype Threat," *Journal of Applied Developmental Psychology* 24, no. 6 (December 2003): 659–60.

5.   Mary Cay Ricci, *Mindsets in the Classroom: Building a Growth Mindset Learning Community* (Waco, TX: Prufrock Press, 2013), 10–11.

6.   Aneeta Rattan, Catherine Good and Carol S. Dweck, "'It's OK—Not Everyone Can Be Good at Math': Instructors with an Entity Theory Comfort (and Demotivate) Students," *Journal of Experimental Social Psychology* 48, no. 3 (May 2012): 36–37.

7.   Teresa Limpo and Rui A. Alves, "Implicit Theories of Writing and their Impact on Students' Response to a SRSD Intervention," *British Journal of Educational Psychology* 84, no. 4 (June 2014): 571–90; Roger Powell, *The Impact of Teacher and Student Mindsets on Responding to Student Writing in First-Year Composition*, (Indiana University of Pennsylvania, 2018); Laura Kate Schubert, *Exploring the Connections Between Students' Mindsets and their Writing: An Intervention Study with a Course-embedded Writing Tutor*, (Indiana University of Pennsylvania, 2017); Sara Hoeve, *Using Mindset Pedagogy to Promote Growth and Increase Efficacy in Student Writers*, (Western Michigan University, 2018).

8.   Natalie Wexler, "Why Americans Can't Write," *The Washington Post* (September 2015).

9   "2017 Writing," *National Assessment of Educational Progress* National Center for Education Statistics, (June 2019). https://nces.ed.gov/nationsreportcard/writing/2017writing.aspx.

10. Frank Pajares and Giovanni Valiante, "Gender Differences in Writing Motivation and Achievement of Middle School Students: A Function of Gender Orientation?" *Contemporary Educational Psychology* 26, no. 3 (July 2001): 171.

11   Roger Bruning and Christy Horn, "Developing Motivation to Write," *Educational Psychologist* 35, no. 1 (March 2000): 5.

12. Limpo and Alves, "Implicit Theories of Writing," 584–85.

13. Laurel Waller and Mostafa Papi, "Motivation and Feedback: How Implicit Theories of Intelligence Predict L2 Writers' Motivation and Feedback Orientation," *Journal of Second Language Writing* 35 (March 2017): 54.

14   Casey Jones, "The Relationship between Writing Centers and Improvement in Writing Ability: An Assessment of the Literature," *Education* 122, no. 1 (September 2001): 9.

15. Michael Palmquist and Richard Young, "The Notion of Giftedness and Student Expectations about Writing," *Written Communication* 9, no. 1 (January 1992): 149–50.

16. Peter Johnston, *Opening Minds: Using Language to Change Lives* (Portsmouth, NH: Stenhouse Publishers, 2012): 21–23.

17. Limpo and Alves, "Implicit Theories of Writing," 579.

18. Nicole Sieben, "Teaching Writing Hope: A Matter of Social Justice in English Education." (Roundtable presentation for the International Federation of the Teaching of English (IFTE)/Conference on English Education (CEE) Conference, Bronx, NY. July 7, 2015); Sieben, *Writing Hope Strategies for Writing Success in Secondary Schools: A Strengths-Based Approach to Teaching Writing* (Leiden, The Netherlands: Brill, 2018): 57.

19. Hoeve, *Using Mindset Pedagogy*, 47–48.

20. Frank Pajares and Giovanni Valiante. "Gender Differences in Writing Motivation and Achievement of Middle School Students: A Function of Gender Orientation?" *Contemporary Educational Psychology* 26, no. 3 (July 2001): 171.

21. National Council of Teachers of English, and National Writing Project, "Framework for Success in Postsecondary Writing," 2011. http://wpacouncil.org/files/ frameworkfor-success-postsecond ary-writing.pdf.

22. Scott Meier, Patricia McCarthy, and Ronald Schmeck, "Validity of Self-Efficacy as a Predictor of Writing Performance," *Cognitive Therapy and Research* 8, no. 2 (April 1984): 117–18; Patricia McCarthy, Scott Meier, and Regina Rinderer, "Self-Efficacy and Writing: A Different View of Self-Evaluation," *College Composition and Communication* 36, no. 4 (December 1985): 469.

23. Laura Kate Schubert, "Exploring the Connections Between Students' Mindsets and Their Writing: An Intervention Study with a Course-Embedded Writing Tutor," PhD diss., Indiana University of Pennsylvania, 2017): 136; Katie E. Schrodt, Amy M. Elleman, Erin R. FitzPatrick, Michelle M. Hasty, Jwa K. Kim, Terri J. Tharp, and Hillary Rector, "An Examination of Mindset Instruction, Self-Regulation, and Writer's Workshop on Kindergarteners' Writing Performance and Motivation: A Mixed-Methods Study," *Reading & Writing Quarterly* 35, no. 5 (May 2019): 440; Hoeve, "\ *Using Mindset Pedagogy*, 107.

24. Katja Upadyaya and Jacquelynne Eccles, "Do Teachers' Perceptions of Children's Math and Reading Related Ability and Effort Predict Children's Self-Concept of Ability in Math and Reading?" *Educational Psychology* 35, no. 1 (January 2015): 123.

25. Joshua Aronson, Carrie B. Fried, and Catherine Good, "Reducing the Effects of Stereotype Threat on African American College Students by Shaping Theories of Intelligence," *Journal of Experimental Social Psychology* 38, no. 2 (March 2002): 123; Good, Aronson, and Inzlicht, "Improving Adolescents' Standardized Test," 658–59.

26. Susana Claro, David Paunesku, and Carol S. Dweck, "Growth Mindset Tempers the Effects of Poverty on Academic Achievement," *Proceedings of the National Academy of Sciences* 113, no. 31 (August 2016): 8667.

27. Ed Week Research Center, "Mindset in the Classroom: A National Study of K–12 Teachers," September 2016, https://www.edweek.org/research-center/mindset-in-the-classroom-a-national-study-of-k-12-teachers.

28. Albert Bandura, "Exercise of Personal and Collective Efficacy in Changing Societies," in *Self-Efficacy in Changing Societies,* ed. Albert Bandura (Cambridge, England: Cambridge University Press, 1997), 2–3.

29. Bandura, "Exercise of Personal," 3.

30. Annie Brock and Heather Hundley, *The Growth Mindset Coach: A Teacher's Month-by-Month Handbook for Empowering Students to Achieve* (Berkeley, CA: Ulysses Press, 2016), 38.

31. Albert Bandura, "Self-Efficacy," in *Encyclopedia of Human Behavior*, vol. 4, ed. Dimitri Ramachaudran (New York: Academic Press, 1994): 71–81.

32. Nancy Sommers, "Revision Strategies of Student Writers and Experienced Adult Writers," *College Composition and Communication* 31, no. 4 (December 1980): 386.

33. Richard Straub, "Responding—Really Responding—to Other Students' Writing," in *The Subject is Writing*, ed. Wendy Bishop (Portsmouth, NH: Heinemann, 1999): 136.

34. Gravity Goldberg, *Mindsets and Moves: Strategies that Help Readers Take Charge* (Thousand Oaks, CA: Corwin, 2016), 39–40.

35. Kelly Gallagher, *In the Best Interest of Students: Staying True to What Works in the ELA Classroom*, (Portsmouth, NH: Stenhouse, 2015), 119–20.

36. Claudia Mueller and Carol S. Dweck, "Praise for Intelligence Can Undermine Children's Motivation and Performance," *Journal of Personality and Social Psychology* 75, no. 1 (July 1998): 33.

37. Donald M. Murray, "The Maker's Eye: Revising Your Own Manuscripts," in *Writing about Writing: A College Reader*, ed. Elizabeth Wardle and Doug Downs (Boston, MA: Bedford/St. Martin's, 2014), 611.

38. Anne Lamott, *Bird by Bird: Some Instructions on Writing and Life* (New York: Anchor, 1994), 25.

39. Lamott, *Bird by Bird,* 25–26.

40. Patrick Rothfuss, "Fanmail Q&A: Revision," https://blog.patrickrothfuss.com/2010/08/fanmail-qa-revision.

41. The *Harry Potter* Lexicon, "JKR: Revision of the plan of Order of the Phoenix," https://www.hp-lexicon. org /source/other-canon/jkr/jkr-com-scrapbook/op-plan.

42. Megan L. Truax, "The Impact of Teacher Language and Growth Mindset Feedback on Writing Motivation," *Literacy Research and Instruction* 57, no. 2 (April 2018): 147.

43. Cheryl Glenn and Melissa Goldthwaile, *St. Martin's Guide to Writing,* 6th ed. (Boston, MA: Bedford/St. Martin's, 2018), 124.

44. Jim Burke, *Teacher's Essential Guide Series: Content Area Writing* (New York, NY: Scholastic Teaching Resources, 2009), 85–86.

45. Penny Kittle, *Write Beside Them: Risk, Voice, and Clarity in High School Writing* (Portsmouth, NH: Heinemann, 2008), 91.

46. Leah Mermelstein, *Self-Directed Writers: The Third Essential Element in the Writing Workshop* (Portsmouth, NH: Heinemann, 2013), 30–35.

47. Kelly Gallagher and Penny Kittle, *180 Days: Two Teachers and the Quest to Engage and Empower Adolescents* (Portsmouth, NH: Heinemann, 2018), 111.

48. Nancie Atwell, *Writing in the Middle.* Companion DVD (Portsmouth, NH: Heinemann, 2014; Kittle, *Write Beside Them*, Companion DVD.

49. Carol Jago, *Papers, Papers, Papers: An English Teacher's Survival Guide* (Portsmouth, NH: Heinemann, 2005), 47, 71, 89, 97.

50. Peter Johnston, *Choice Words: How Our Language Affects Children's Learning* (Portsmouth, NH: Stenhouse, 2004), 31.

51. Kristine Mraz and Christine Hertz, *A Mindset for Learning: Teaching the Traits of Joyful, Independent Growth* (Portsmouth, NH: Heinemann, 2015), 57.

52. Carol S. Dweck, "The Power of Believing That You Can Improve" TED Talk (2014) https://youtu.be/_XOmgOOSpLU.

53. Annie Brock and Heather Hundley, *The Growth Mindset Playbook: A Teacher's Guide to Promoting Student Success* (Berkeley, CA: Ulysses Press, 2017), 21–23.

54. Sara Hoeve, *180 Ready-to-Use Growth Mindset Prompts* (Auburn Hills, MI: Teacher's Discovery, 2019).

55. Kittle, *Write Beside Them*, 92.

56. Lamott, *Bird by Bird*, 22.

57. Malcolm X., *The Autobiography of Malcolm X.,* ed. Alex Haley (New York, NY: Ballantine, 1965) excerpt at http://accounts.smccd.edu/bellr/readerlearningtoread.htm; Elizabeth Kiefer, "J.K. Rowling Shares Two Post-Harry Potter Rejection Letters with Fans," *Refinery* 29. March 25, 2016, https://www.refinery29.com/en-us/2016/03/106877/j-k-rowling-rejection-letters.

58. Victor Villanueva, *Bootstraps: From an Academic of Color* (Urbana, IL: NCTE, 1993; Sherman Alexie, "The Joy of Reading and Writing: Superman and Me," in *The Most Wonderful Books: Writers on Discovering the Pleasures of Reading* (Minneapolis, MN: Milkweed Editions, 1997); Maya Angelou, "Graduation," https://www.cbsd.org/cms/lib/PA01916442/Centricity/Domain/1574/Graduation%20Text.pdf; Elaine Richardson, "My Ill Literacy Narrative: Growing Up Black, Po and a Girl, In the Hood," *Gender and Education* 21, no. 6 (November 2009); Jason Birchmeier, "Nas – Biography," *AllMusic*. https://www.allmusic.com/artist/nas-mn0000373634/biography.

59. "Michael Jordan's 'Failure' Nike Commercial," *YouTube* https://www.youtube.com/watch?v=JA7G7AV-LT8; "Dick & Rick Hoyt," *YouTube* https://www.youtube.com/watch?v=dDnrLv6z-mM.

60. "Famous Failures," images found at https://cmoe.com/blog/famous-failures, https://www.oberlo.com/blog/famous-failures, https://chesschristian.wordpress.com/2016/06/22/famous-failures.

61. "Formerly Homeless Nigerian Refugee Is Now a Chess National Master at the Age of 10," *Upworthy*, https://scoop.upworthy.com/formerly-homeless-nigerian-refugee-now-chess-national-master-10-year-old.

62. *Pass It On*, https://www.passiton.com.

63. Tony Wagner and Ted Dintersmith, *Most Likely to Succeed: Preparing Our Kids for the Innovation Era* (New York: Scribner, 2015), 206.

64. Dweck, *Mindset*, 201.

65. The Princeton Review, "What Looks Good on College Applications?" https://www.princetonreview.com/college -advice/what-looks-good-on-college-applications.

66. Common Core State Standards Initiative, "English Language Arts Standards," http://www.corestandard s.org /ELA-Literacy.

67. Dale Frost, "Competency Works Releases Updated Competency Education State Policy Map," *Aurora Institute,* June 21, 2018, https://aurora-institute.org/blog/competencyworks-releases-updated-competency-education-state-policy-map-for-the-united-states.

68. Brock and Hundley, *The Growth Mindset Playbook*, 130.

69. Lisa Fink, "Beliefs about the Teaching of Writing," *NCTE,* May 9, 2015, https://ncte.org/blog/2015/05/beliefs-about-the-teaching-of-writing.

70. David S. Yeager, Paul Hanselman, Gregory Walton, Jared S. Murray, Robert Crosnoe, Chandra Muller, Elizabeth Tipton et al, "A National Experiment Reveals

Where a Growth Mindset Improves Achievement," *Nature* 573, no. 7774 (2019): 364–65.

71. Lydia Denworth, "Debate Arises over Teaching 'Growth Mindsets' to Motivate Students," Scientific American (2019) https://www.scientificamerican.com/article/debate-arises-over-teaching-growth-mindsets-to-motivate-students.

72. Mraz and Hertz, A Mindset for Learning, 128.

BIBLIOGRAPHY

Andersen, Simon, and Helena Nielsen. "Reading Intervention with a Growth Mindset Approach Improves Children's Skills." *Proceedings of the National Academy of Sciences* 113, no. 43 (October 2016): 12111–13.

Aronson, Joshua, Carrie B. Fried, and Catherine Good. "Reducing the Effects of Stereotype Threat on African American College Students by Shaping Theories of Intelligence." *Journal of Experimental Social Psychology* 38, no. 2 (March 2002): 113–25.

Atwell, Nancie. *Writing in the Middle: New Understandings about Writing, Reading, and Learning.* Portsmouth, NH: Boyton/Cook, 1998.

Bandura, Albert. "Exercise of Personal and Collective Efficacy in Changing Societies." In *Self-Efficacy in Changing Societies*, edited by Albert Bandura, 1–45. Cambridge, England: Cambridge University Press, 1997.

Blackwell, Lisa S., Kali H. Trzesniewski, and Carol S. Dweck. "Implicit Theories of Intelligence Predict Achievement across an Adolescent Transition: A Longitudinal Study and an Intervention." *Child Development* 78, no. 1 (January 2007): 246–63.

Boaler, Jo. "Ability and Mathematics: The Mindset Revolution that is Reshaping Education." *Forum* 55, no. 1 (March 2013): 143–46.

Boaler, Jo. *Mathematical Mindsets: Unleashing Students' Potential through Creative Math, Inspiring Messages and Innovative Teaching.* San Francisco, CA: Jossey-Bass, 2015.

Brock, Annie, and Heather Hundley. *The Growth Mindset Coach: A Teacher's Month-by-Month Handbook for Empowering Students to Achieve.* Berkeley, CA: Ulysses Press, 2016.

Brock, Annie, and Heather Hundley. *The Growth Mindset Playbook: A Teacher's Guide to Promoting Student Success*. Berkeley, CA: Ulysses Press, 2017.

Broda, Michael, John Yun, Barbara Schneider, David S. Yeager, Gregory M. Walton, and Matthew Diemer. "Reducing Inequality in Academic Success for Incoming College Students: A Randomized Trial of Growth Mindset and Belonging Interventions." *Journal of Research on Educational Effectiveness* 11, no. 3 (July 2018): 317–38.

Brougham, Lisa, and Susan Kashubeck-West. "Impact of a Growth Mindset Intervention on Academic Performance of Students at Two Urban High Schools." *Professional School Counseling* 21, no. 1 (2017): 2156759X18764934.

Bruning, Roger, and Christy Horn. "Developing Motivation to Write." *Educational Psychologist* 35, no. 1 (March 2000): 25–37.

Burnette, Jeni L., V. Michelle Russell, Crystal L. Hoyt, Kasey Orvidas, and Laura Widman. "An Online Growth Mindset Intervention in a Sample of Rural Adolescent Girls." *British Journal of Educational Psychology* 88, no. 3 (September 2018): 428–45.

Burnette, Jeni L., Jeffrey M. Pollack, and Crystal L. Hoyt. "Individual Differences in Implicit Theories of Leadership Ability and Self-Efficacy: Predicting Responses to Stereotype Threat." *Journal of Leadership Studies* 3, no. 4 (December 2010): 46–56.

Claro, Susana, David Paunesku, and Carol S. Dweck. "Growth Mindset Tempers the Effects of Poverty on Academic Achievement." *Proceedings of the National Academy of Sciences* 113, no. 31 (August 2016): 8664–68.

Costa, Arthur, Robert Garmston, Carolee Hayes, and Jane Ellison. *Cognitive Coaching: Developing Self-Directed Leaders and Learners*. 3rd ed. Washington D.C.: Rowman & Littlefield, 2015.

Denworth, Lydia. "Debate Arises over Teaching 'Growth Mindsets' to Motivate Students." *Scientific American* (2019).

Duckworth, Angela. *Grit: The Power of Passion and Perseverance*. New York, NY: Scribner, 2016.

Dweck, Carol S., Chi-yue Chiu, and Ying-yi Hong. "Implicit Theories and Their Role in Judgments and Reactions: A Word from Two Perspectives." *Psychological Inquiry* 6, no. 4 (1995): 267–85.

Dweck, Carol S., and Daniel C. Molden. "Self-theories: Their Impact on Competence Motivation and Acquisition." In *Handbook of Competence and Motivation*, edited by Andrew J. Elliot and Carol S. Dweck, 122–40. New York: Guilford Press, 2005.

Dweck, Carol S., and Ellen Leggett. "A Social Cognitive Approach to Motivation and Personality." *Psychological Review* 95, no. 2 (April 1988): 256–73.

Dweck, Carol S. *Mindset: The New Psychology of Success*. New York: Ballantine Books, 2006.

Dweck, Carol S. "The Perils and Promises of Praise." ASCD 65, no. 2 (2007): 34–39.

Dweck, Carol S. *Self-theories: Their Role in Motivation, Personality, and Development*. Philadelphia, PA: Taylor and Francis/Psychology Press, 1999.

Esparza, Julie, Lee Shumow, and Jennifer Schmidt. "Growth Mindset of Gifted Seventh Grade Students in Science." *NCSSSMST Journal* 19, no. 1 (2014): 6–13.

Fillmore, Erin, and Robert Helfenbein. "Medical Student Grit and Performance in Gross Anatomy: What Are the Relationships?" *FASEB Journal* 29, no. 1 supplement (April 2015): 689–96.

Flower, Linda, and John R. Hayes, "A Cognitive Process Theory of Writing." *College Composition and Communication* 32, no. 4 (December 1981): 365–87.

Gallagher, Kelly, and Penny Kittle. *180 Days: Two Teachers and the Quest to Engage and Empower Adolescents*. Portsmouth, NH: Heinemann, 2018.

Gallagher, Kelly. *In the Best Interest of Students: Staying True to What Works in the ELA Classroom*. Portsmouth, NH: Stenhouse, 2015.

Gandhi, Jill, Tyler W. Watts, Michael D. Masucci, and C. Cybele Raver. "The Effects of Two Mindset Interventions on Low-Income Students' Academic and Psychological Outcomes." *Journal of Research on Educational Effectiveness* 13, no. 2 (April 2020): 351–79.

Ganimian, Alejandro J. "Growth-Mindset Interventions at Scale: Experimental Evidence from Argentina." *Educational Evaluation and Policy Analysis* 42, no. 3 (September 2020): 417–38.

Gillespie, Amy, Natalie G. Olinghouse, and Steve Graham. "Fifth-Grade Students' Knowledge about Writing Process and Writing Genres." *The Elementary School Journal* 113, no. 4 (June 2013): 565–88.

Glenn, Cheryl, and Melissa Goldthwaile. *St. Martin's Guide to Writing*. 6th ed. Boston, MA: Bedford/St. Martin's, 2018.

Goldberg, Gravity. *Mindsets and Moves: Strategies that Help Readers Take Charge*. Thousand Oaks, CA: Corwin, 2015.

Good, Catherine, Aneeta Rattan, and Carol S. Dweck. "Why Do Women Opt Out? Sense of Belonging and Women's Representation in Mathematics." *Journal of Personality and Social Psychology* 102, no. 4 (April 2012): 700–17.

Good, Catherine, Joshua Aronson, and Michael Inzlicht. "Improving Adolescents' Standardized Test Performance: An Intervention to Reduce the Effects of Stereotype Threat." *Journal of Applied Developmental Psychology* 24, no. 6 (December 2003): 645–62.

Graham, Steve, Shirley Schwartz, and Charles MacArthur. "Knowledge of Writing and the Composing Process, Attitude toward Writing, and Self-efficacy for Students with and without Learning Disabilities." *Journal of Learning Disabilities* 26, no. 4 (April 1993): 237–49.

Graham, Steve, Karen Harris, Barbara Fink, and Charles MacArthur. "Teacher Efficacy in Writing: A Construct Validation with Primary Grade Teachers." *Scientific Studies of Reading* 5, no. 2 (November): 177–202.

Graham, Steve, Virginia Berninger, and Weihua Fan. "The Structural Relationship between Writing Attitude and Writing Achievement in First and Third Grade Students." *Contemporary Educational Psychology* 32, no. 3 (July 2007): 516–36.

Graham, Steve, Virginia Berninger, and Robert Abbott. "Are Attitudes toward Writing and Reading Separable Constructs? A Study with Primary Grade Children." *Reading & Writing Quarterly* 28, no. 1 (January 2012): 51–69.

Grant, Heidi, and Carol S. Dweck. "Clarifying Achievement Goals and Their Impact." *Journal of Personality and Social Psychology* 85, no. 3 (September 2003): 541–53.

Gutshall, Anne C. "Student Perceptions of Teachers' Mindset Beliefs in the Classroom Setting." *Journal of Educational and Developmental Psychology* 6, no. 2 (July 2016): 135–42.

Hattie, John. "Misinterpreting the Growth Mindset: Why We're Doing Students a Disservice." *Education Week* (2017).

Heine, Steven, Shinobu Kitayama, Darrin Lehman, Toshitake Takata, Eugene Ide, Cecilia Leung, Hisaya Matsumoto, and Patricia Devine. "Divergent Motivational Consequences of Success and Failure in Japan and North America." *Journal of Personality and Social Psychology* 81, no. 4 (October 2001): 599–615.

Heyman, Gail, and Carol S. Dweck. "Achievement Goals and Intrinsic Motivation: Their Relation and their Role in Adaptive Motivation." *Motivation and Emotion* 16, no. 3 (September 1992): 231–47.

Hochanadel, Aaron, and Dora Finamore. "Fixed and Growth Mindset in Education and How Grit Helps Students Persist in the Face of Adversity." *Journal of International Education Research* 11, no. 1, (January 2015): 47–50.

Hoeve, Sara. *180 Ready-to-Use Growth Mindset Prompts*. Auburn Hills, MI: Teacher's Discovery, 2019.

Hoeve, Sara. *Using Mindset Pedagogy to Promote Growth and Increase Efficacy in Student Writers*. Western Michigan University, 2018.

Jago, Carol. *Papers, Papers, Papers: An English Teacher's Survival Guide*. Portsmouth, NH: Heinemann, 2005.

Johnston, Peter. *Choice Words: How Our Language Affects Children's Learning*. Portsmouth, NH: Stenhouse Publishers, 2004.

Johnston, Peter. *Opening Minds: Using Language to Change Lives*. Portsmouth, NH: Stenhouse Publishers, 2012.

Jones, Casey. "The Relationship between Writing Centers and Improvement in Writing Ability: An Assessment of the Literature." *Education* 122, no. 1 (September 2001): 3–21.

Kittle, Penny. *Write Beside Them: Risk, Voice and Clarity in High School Writing*. Portsmouth, NH: Heinemann, 2008.

Lamott, Anne. *Bird by Bird: Some Instructions on Writing and Life*. New York: Anchor, 1994.

Limpo, Teresa, and Rui A. Alves. "Implicit Theories of Writing and their Impact on Students' Response to a SRSD Intervention." *British Journal of Educational Psychology* 84, no. 4 (June 2014): 571–90.

Nigel, Mantou Lou, and Kimberly A. Noels. "Changing Language Mindsets: Implications for Goal Orientations and Responses to Failure In and Outside the Second Language Classroom." *Contemporary Educational Psychology* 46 (July 2016): 22–33.

McCarthy, Patricia, Scott Meier, and Regina Rinderer. "Self-Efficacy and Writing: A Different View of Self-Evaluation." *College Composition and Communication* 36, no. 4 (December 1985): 465–71.

Meier, Scott, Patricia McCarthy, and Ronald Schmeck. "Validity of Self-Efficacy as a Predictor of Writing Performance." *Cognitive Therapy and Research* 8, no. 2 (April 1984): 107–20.

Mercer, Sarah, and Stephen Ryan. "A Mindset for EFL: Learners' Beliefs about the Role of Natural Talent." *ELT Journal* 64, no. 4 (October 2010): 436–44.

Mermelstein, Leah. *Self-Directed Writers: The Third Essential Element in the Writing Workshop*. Portsmouth, NH: Heinemann, 2013.

Molden, Daniel C., and Carol S. Dweck. "Finding 'Meaning' in Psychology: A Lay Theories Approach to Self-Regulation, Social Perception, and Social Development." *American Psychologist* 61, no. 3 (April 2006): 192–203.

Mraz, Kristine, and Christine Hertz. *A Mindset for Learning: Teaching the Traits of Joyful, Independent Growth*. Portsmouth, NH: Heinemann, 2015.

Mueller, Claudia, and Carol S. Dweck. "Praise for Intelligence Can Undermine Children's Motivation and Performance." *Journal of Personality and Social Psychology* 75, no. 1 (July 1998): 33–52.

Murray, Donald M. "The Maker's Eye: Revising Your Own Manuscripts." In *Writing about Writing: A College Reader*. 2nd ed. Edited by Elizabeth Wardle and Doug Downs, 610–14. Boston, MA: Bedford/St. Martin's, 2014.

Nishida, Tamotsu. "Achievement Motivation for Learning in Physical Education Class: A Cross-Cultural Study in Four Countries." *Perceptual and Motor Skills*, 72 no. 3 (June 1991): 1183–86.

Olson, Kristina R., and Carol S. Dweck. "A Blueprint for Social Cognitive Development." *Perspectives on Psychological Science* 3, no. 3 (May 2008): 193–202.

Orosz, Gábor, Szlivia Péter-Szarka, Beáta Bőthe, István Tóth-Király, and Rony Berger. "How Not to Do a Mindset Intervention: Learning From a Mindset Intervention among Students with Good Grades." *Frontiers in Psychology* 8 (March 2017): 1–11.

Orvidas, Kasey, Jeni Burnette, Jessica Schleider, Joseph Skelton, Melissa Moses, and Julie Dunsmore. "Healthy Body, Healthy Mind: A Mindset Intervention for Obese Youth." *The Journal of Genetic Psychology* 181, no. 6 (February 2020): 443–57.

Outes-León, Ingo, Alan Sánchez, and Renos Vakis. *The Power of Believing You Can Get Smarter: The Impact of a Growth-Mindset Intervention on Academic Achievement in Peru*. The World Bank, 2020.

Pajares, Frank, and Giovanni Valiante. "Gender Differences in Writing Motivation and Achievement of Middle School Students: A Function of Gender Orientation?" *Contemporary Educational Psychology* 26, no. 3 (July 2001): 366–81.

Pajares, Frank, and Margaret Johnson. "Self-Efficacy Beliefs and the Writing Performance of Entering High School Students." *Psychology in the Schools* 33, no. 2 (April 1996): 163–75.

Pajares, Frank. "Self-Efficacy Beliefs, Motivation, and Achievement in Writing: A Review of the Literature." *Reading & Writing Quarterly* 19 (April 2003): 139–58.

Palmquist, Michael, and Richard Young. "The Notion of Giftedness and Student Expectations about Writing." *Written Communication* 9, no. 1 (January 1992): 138–68.

Parada, Sacha, and Jean-François Verlhiac. "Growth Mindset Intervention among French Students, and its Articulation with Proactive Coping Strategies." *Educational Psychology* (May 2021): 1–20.

Pintrich, Paul. "A Conceptual Framework for Assessing Motivation and Self-Regulated Learning in College Students." *Educational Psychology Review* 16, no. 4 (December 2004): 385–407.

Powell, Roger. *The Impact of Teacher and Student Mindsets on Responding to Student Writing in First-Year Composition*. Indiana University of Pennsylvania, 2018.

Rege, Mari, Paul Hanselman, Ingeborg Foldøy Solli, Carol S. Dweck, Sten Ludvigsen, Eric Bettinger, Robert Crosnoe, Chandra Muller, Gregory Walton, Angela Duckworth, and David S. Yeager. "How Can We Inspire Nations of Learners? An Investigation of Growth Mindset and Challenge-Seeking in Two Countries." *American Psychologist* (November 2020).

Ricci, Mary Cay. *Mindsets in the Classroom: Building a Growth Mindset Learning Community*. Waco, TX: Prufrock Press, 2013.

Rattan, Aneeta, Catherine Good, and Carol S. Dweck. "'It's OK—Not Everyone Can Be Good at Math': Instructors with an Entity Theory Comfort (and Demotivate) Students." *Journal of Experimental Social Psychology* 48, no. 3 (May 2012): 731–37.

Schimmer, Tom, Garnet Hillman, and Mandy Stalets. *Standards-Based Learning in Action*. Bloomington, IN: Solution Tree, 2018.

Schleider, Jessica, and John Weisz. "A Single-Session Growth Mindset Intervention for Adolescent Anxiety and Depression: 9-Month Outcomes of a Randomized Trial." *Journal of Child Psychology and Psychiatry* 59, no. 2 (February 2018): 160–70.

Schleider, Jessica, Michael Mullarkey, and John Weisz. "Protocol for a Three-Arm Randomized Trial of Virtual Reality and Web-based Growth Mindset Interventions for Adolescent Depression." *JMIR Research Protocols* 8, no. 7 (July 2019): e13368.

Schmidt, Jennifer, Lee Shumow, and Hayal Kackar-Cam. "Does Mindset Intervention Predict Students' Daily Experience in Classrooms? A Comparison of Seventh and Ninth Graders' Trajectories." *Journal of Youth and Adolescence* 46, no. 3 (March 2017): 582–602.

Schrodt, Katie E., Amy M. Elleman, Erin R. FitzPatrick, Michelle M. Hasty, Jwa K. Kim, Terri J. Tharp, and Hillary Rector. "An Examination of Mindset Instruction, Self-Regulation, and Writer's Workshop on Kindergarteners' Writing Performance and Motivation: A Mixed-Methods Study." *Reading & Writing Quarterly* 35, no. 5 (May 2019): 427–44.

Schubert, Laura Kate. *Exploring the Connections Between Students' Mindsets and their Writing: An Intervention Study with a Course-Embedded Writing Tutor*. Indiana University of Pennsylvania, 2017.

Shell, Duane, Carolyn C. Murphy, and Roger H. Bruning. "Self-Efficacy and Outcome Expectancy Mechanisms in Reading and Writing Achievement." *Journal of Educational Psychology* 81, no. 1 (March 1989): 91–100.

Sieben, Nicole. "Teaching Writing Hope: A Matter of Social Justice in English Education." Roundtable presentation for the International Federation of the Teaching of English (IFTE)/Conference on English Education (CEE) Conference, Bronx, NY. July 7, 2015.

Sieben, Nicole. *Writing Hope Strategies for Writing Success in Secondary Schools: A Strengths-Based Approach to Teaching Writing*. Leiden, The Netherlands: Brill, 2018.

Sommers, Nancy. "Revision Strategies of Student Writers and Experienced Adult Writers." *College Composition and Communication* 31, no. 4 (December 1980): 378–88.

Sriram, Rishi. "Rethinking Intelligence: The Role of Mindset in Promoting Success for Academically High-Risk Students." *Journal of College Student Retention: Research, Theory & Practice* 15, no. 4 (February 2014): 515–36.

Straub, Richard. "Responding—Really Responding—to Other Students' Writing." In *The Subject is Writing*, edited by Wendy Bishop, 136–146. Portsmouth, NH: Heinemann, 1999.

Thordardottir, Elin. "Language Intervention from a Bilingual Mindset." *ASHA Leader* 11, no. 10 (August 2006): 6–21.

Truax, Megan L. "The Impact of Teacher Language and Growth Mindset Feedback on Writing Motivation." *Literacy Research and Instruction* 57, no. 2 (April 2018): 135–157.

Upadyaya, Katja, and Jacquelynne Eccles. "Do Teachers' Perceptions of Children's Math and Reading Related Ability and Effort Predict Children's Self-Concept of Ability in Math and Reading?" *Educational Psychology* 35, no. 1 (January 2015): 110–27.

Verberg, Fenneke, Petra Helmond, and Geertjan Overbeek. "Study Protocol: A Randomized Controlled Trial Testing the Effectiveness of an Online Mindset Intervention in Adolescents with Intellectual Disabilities." *BMC Psychiatry* 18, no. 1 (December 2018): 1–12.

Wagner, Tony, and Ted Dintersmith. *Most Likely to Succeed: Preparing Our Kids for the Innovation Era*. New York, NY: Scribner, 2015.

Waller, Laurel, and Mostafa Papi. "Motivation and Feedback: How Implicit Theories of Intelligence Predict L2 Writers' Motivation and Feedback Orientation." *Journal of Second Language Writing* 35 (March 2017): 54–65.

Wanzek, Jeanne, Stephanie Al Otaiba, Yaacov Petscher, Christopher Lemmons, Samantha Gessel, Sally Fluhler, Rachel Donegan, and Brenna Rivas. "Comparing the Effects of Reading Intervention Versus Reading and Mindset Intervention for Upper Elementary Students with Reading Difficulties." *Journal of Learning Disabilities* 54, no. 3 (May 2021): 203–20.

Yeager, David S., and Carol S. Dweck. "Mindsets that Promote Resilience: When Students Believe that Personal Characteristics can be Developed." *Educational Psychologist* 47, no. 4 (October 2012): 302–14.

Yeager, David S., and Gregory Walton. "Social-Psychological Interventions in Education: They're Not Magic." *Review of Educational Research* 81, no. 2 (June 2011): 267–301.

Yeager, David S., Paul Hanselman, Gregory Walton, Jared S. Murray, Robert Crosnoe, Chandra Muller, Elizabeth Tipton et al. "A National Experiment Reveals Where a Growth Mindset Improves Achievement." *Nature* 573, no. 7774 (September 2019): 364–69.

Yeager, David S., Kali Trzesniewski, Kirsi Tirri, Petri Nokelainen, and Carol S. Dweck. "Adolescents' Implicit Theories Predict Desire for Vengeance after Remembered and Hypothetical Peer Conflicts: Correlational and Experimental Evidence." *Developmental Psychology* 47, no. 4 (2011): 1090–1107.

Yeager, David S., Kali Trzesniewski, and Carol S. Dweck. "An Implicit Theories of Personality Intervention Reduces Adolescent Aggression in Response to Victimization and Exclusion." *Child Development* 84, no. 3 (May 2013): 970–88.

Zhu, Pei, Ivonne Garcia, Kate Boxer, Sidhant Wadhera, and Erick Alonzo. "Using a Growth Mindset Intervention to Help Ninth-Graders: An Independent Evaluation of the National Study of Learning Mindsets." *MDRC* (November 2019).

ACKNOWLEDGMENTS

Thank you to Ulysses Press and my project editor, Renee Rutledge, for helping me transform over a decade of conversations and classroom moments into actionable teaching strategies.

I would like to acknowledge the researchers whose work serves as a foundation for this book, most notably Carol Dweck, Frank Pajares, and Albert Bandura. Mary Cay Ricci is also an important influence, as her book *Mindsets in the Classroom* sparked my inquiry into the intersections between student mindsets and their beliefs about writing.

As shown by the references throughout this book, my classroom beliefs and practices have been shaped by many great writing teachers, especially Don Murray, Penny Kittle, Kelly Gallagher, Jim Burke, Anne Lamott, and Carole Jago.

Thank you to Jonathan Bush, my mentor and friend, for indulging me in hours of conversation about writing mindset pedagogy. Over the years, you have taught me about research, pedagogy, and teacher education, but also about resilience, grace, and balance.

I am grateful for the superwomen in my life, who pursue their passions and professional goals, while still prioritizing their friends and family—Jill

Veeneman, Megan Vollink, Tara Star Johnson, Thelma Ensink, and Steffany Comfort Maher.

My deepest appreciation is for my family. My husband, Mitch, demonstrates a saintly patience and unwavering support for my career. Thank you for stepping in to help every time that I needed to write or grade. I could not imagine a better partner in life. I am thankful for the support of my parents. They will never teach writing, but will still be the first in line to read this book. And my children, Grace, Austin, and Jackson. Thank you for cheering me on. My cup continues to overflow.

Finally, I am indebted to the hundreds of students who have shared their writing with me over the last decade. It has been an honor to read your words and walk alongside of you as you tried, failed, learned, and grew!

ABOUT THE AUTHOR

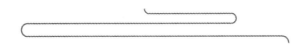

Dr. Sara Hoeve is a former high school English teacher with over fifteen years of experience teaching writing in secondary and college classrooms. She has worked as an instructional coach and writing consultant, supporting both pre-service and practicing teachers. Dr. Hoeve is currently the Director of Student Teaching and Teacher Certification at Hope College. She also teaches pedagogy courses at Purdue University. Dr. Hoeve serves as the cochair of the ELATE Commission on Writing Teacher Education, and continues to lead workshops on mindset pedagogy at state and national conferences. She lives in Hudsonville, Michigan, with her husband Mitch and their three children.